THE  BOOK OF
FOOTBALL
QUOTATIONS

THE 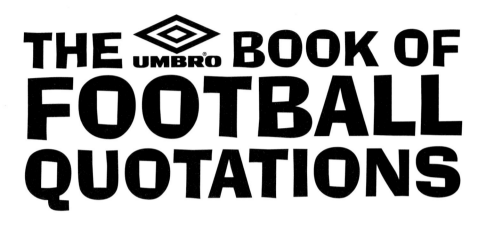 BOOK OF FOOTBALL QUOTATIONS

Peter Ball and Phil Shaw

EBURY PRESS
LONDON

First published 1996

© Peter Ball and Phil Shaw

Peter Ball and Phil Shaw have asserted their right under
the Copyright, Designs and Patents Act 1988 to be iden-
tified as the authors of this work

First published in the United Kingdom
in 1996 by Ebury Press, Random House,
20 Vauxhall Bridge Road, London SW1V 2SA

Random House Australia (Pty) Limited
20 Alfred Street, Milsons Point, Sydney,
New South Wales 2061, Australia

Random House New Zealand Limited
18 Poland Road, Glenfield
Auckland 10, New Zealand

Random House South Africa (Pty) Limited
PO Box 2263, Rosebank 2121, South Africa

Random House UK Limited Reg No. 954009

A CIP catalogue record for this book
is available from the British Library

3 5 7 9 10 8 6 4

ISBN 0 09 180887 1

Designed by Roger Walker/Graham Harmer

Printed and bound in Great Britain by
BPC Hazells Ltd, Aylesbury, Bucks.

ACKNOWLEDGEMENTS

The publishers would like to thank the following for permission to
reproduce the photographs used in this book.

Cover pictures: Allsport, Action Images, Empics.
Colour plate section: Professional Sport (plates 1, 2, 3, 6, 7);
Allsport (plates 4, 5, 8, 9, 10, 11, 12, 13, 14, 15, 16, 17).
Black and white photographs: Action Images (pages 4, 15, 24, 34, 44,
51, 53, 69, 80, 90, 112, 168); Allsport (pages 123, 136, 152, 175).

Contents

Acknowledgements

This book, the fifth edition of the *Book of Football Quotations* and the second with the prestigious support of UMBRO, would not have existed without the efforts of hundreds of others.

Our first thanks are to the players, managers, fans and officials whose utterances made it all possible, and especially to those journalists who waited in a rainy street or crowded corridor after a match to record their comments. They are too numerous to mention, but every reporter, whether in the national or local media, can take our appreciation as read.

We are particularly indebted for their contributions and interest to a cast of dozens including Len Capeling, Andy Colquhoun, Christopher Davies, Jonathan Foster, Brian Glanville, Tony Leighton, Chris Maume, Kenny Mac-Donald, Kevin McCarra, Glenn Moore, Dennis Shaw, Adrian Thrills, Steve Tongue and Henry Winter.

Peter Ball, Lancashire
Phil Shaw, Staffordshire
Summer, 1996

CHAPTER 1

The Greats and Others

Players

TONY ADAMS

I'll never forget the day he was sent to prison for drink driving. Just after he was sentenced, he whispered to me: 'I have done wrong and I'm going to take the punishment. I don't want to appeal'. That's Tony. If you're in a battle on the pitch, he's the first bloke you'd want on your side.

DAVID O'LEARY, former Arsenal team-mate, 1995.

Strange how his image is frozen in the mind: pushing up, bawling at the nearest linesman and jabbing his right arm at the sky. If ever Adams had the misfortune to pull a shoulder muscle, you feel his career might seize up overnight.

PATRICK COLLINS, columnist, *Mail on Sunday*, 1994.

PHILIPPE ALBERT

We tried everything to get him. Maybe they offered Sharon Stone.

OSSIE ARDILES, Tottenham manager, on losing the Belgian defender to Newcastle, 1994.

DANIEL AMOKACHI

He is built like an ebony outhouse.

PATRICK BARCLAY, football correspondent, *The Observer*, 1995.

CHRIS ARMSTRONG

When I try to speak to him about his future, he tells me to talk to his agent. Well, it's not his agent he rings when the car won't start or the baby has earache. It is me or my wife at two in the morning.

ALAN SMITH, Crystal Palace manager, on problems with his striker, 1995.

To say that I don't try was way wide of the mark. I give my all in every game. I know how lucky I am to be here. I used to get up at six in the morning to pack beefburgers in a factory in Wrexham.

ARMSTRONG, Spurs striker, on the suggestion by Smith that he lacked the 'hunger to succeed', 1995.

FAUSTINO ASPRILLA

He's a real Newcastle player – quick, works hard, and has flair – the sort of player that Geordies love.

KEVIN KEEGAN, Newcastle manager, on paying £7m for the Colombian, 1996.

He's from Latin America – that's the way they are.

KEEGAN, after Asprilla was accused of elbowing and butting Manchester City's Keith Curle, 1996.

PHIL BABB

Arguably the guy with the most lusted-after legs in British football.

LISA I'ANSON, compere, BBC-TV show *Dear Dilemma*, 1995.

There were 10 of us who used to knock around together in Streatham. At the last count, only two of us were on the outside (of jail). Football was my way out and that was my good fortune.

BABB, Liverpool defender, 1994.

ROBERTO BAGGIO

The Divine Pony Tail

ITALIAN FANS' BANNER, World Cup finals, 1994.

JOHN BARNES

I wish I'd been as dedicated at 24 as I am now. I'd have trained more, kept out of McDonald's, got some early nights.

> BARNES, Liverpool and England mid fielder, at the age of 31, 1995.

There's always women after him. We've got through a couple of nannies. They're fine with me but as soon as they see John they go to pieces. One started off mousy brown, but after a few weeks strolling round in tight mini-skirts I got rid of her.

> SUSIE BARNES, wife, 1995.

WARREN BARTON

The best-dressed footballer I've ever seen. Even in training – we're all in tracksuits and he arrives in shirt, trousers and shoes. And his hair's lovely. We call him The Dog, as in the dog's bollocks.

> ROBERT LEE, Newcastle mid fielder, telling *Goal* magazine about his club colleague, 1996.

PETER BEARDSLEY

I'd pay money to watch him train.

> JIMMY GABRIEL, Everton caretaker manager, 1993.

He's having a home built in the area. If I had my way I'd build a big wall round it and put in guard dogs to stop him leaving.

> KEVIN KEEGAN, Newcastle manager, 1994.

Life's a compromise. I had to compromise over Beardsley. I thought he was too old, and that the money Kevin Keegan wanted to spend on him was going down the drain.

> SIR JOHN HALL, Newcastle chairman, 1995.

I often get called Quasimodo and have done for nine years. But the way I look at it is that if I was in those fans' colours, they'd be happy with me.

> BEARDSLEY, 1995.

I NEVER BELIEVED IN STAR STATUS. THAT TO ME MEANS ROLEX WATCHES, GOLD CHAINS AND FLASHY CARS. I HATE ALL OF THESE.

DENNIS BERGKAMP pictured with Arsenal manager Bruce Rioch, 1995.

He's the only player who, when he appears on TV, Daleks hide behind the sofa.

NICK HANCOCK, compere, on the BBC-TV show
They Think It's All Over, 1995.

Dennis Bergkamp

If he thinks he's going to set the world alight he can forget it. When the fog, ice and cold arrive, he won't want to know.

ALAN SUGAR, Tottenham chairman, after the Dutchman's £7.25m
move to Arsenal, 1995.

George Best

I'd be worth around £14m to £15m by today's prices.

BEST, 1996.

People say he wasted his career. Nonsense. He was hunted down by defenders for 11 full seasons, starting at 17. He paid his dues all right.

DAVID MEEK, journalist, who covered Manchester United
for 37 years, on retiring, 1995.

Over the last few years I've lost a lot of friends at a very young age and yet I was the one they kept saying wouldn't make 30, wouldn't make 40, wouldn't make 50. And I'm still here.

BEST, at 49, 1995.

I didn't believe in love at first sight until I met Alex. She is fabulous and I feel like a kid again. People will say it's just George being George again, but she means everything to me.

BEST, on marrying a 23-year-old air hostess on his 49th birthday, 1995.

Steve Bruce

But why was he trying to convince the FA he should be shown some leniency - because he looks like Bernard Cribbins?

BRIAN McCLAIR, Manchester United midfielder, in his 'Life of Brian' column,
United Magazine, 1995.

STEVE BULL

He's the best goal scorer I've ever played with. He's so single-minded. I've known some greedy players – I remember wrestling for the ball with Gavin Peacock, who's in Christians in Sport for heaven's sake, when Newcastle had a penalty and I was on a hat-trick – but Bully takes the biscuit.

DAVID KELLY, Wolves striker, 1994.

JOHN BURRIDGE

When I came into the game as a 15-year-old, one of the trainers said to me: 'Son, goalkeepers have got to be crackers and daft. You son, have got the qualities of an international'. I took it as a compliment.

BURRIDGE, eccentric veteran goalkeeper, 1994.

I've even known him to give an interview to Gerald Sinstadt in his sleep.

JANET BURRIDGE, wife, 1994.

ERIC CANTONA

When Eric feels an injustice, he has to prove to the whole world that he's been wronged. He can't control his temper. That's just part of his game.

ALEX FERGUSON, Manchester United manager, after Cantona's dismissal
in a pre-season friendly against Rangers, 1994.

Nothing more than a brat.

JIMMY HILL, BBC-TV after Cantona's back kick at
Norwich's John Polston, 1994.

Nothing will ever make me wiser, and there's nothing I need to be wiser about. What I mean is that there are bad sides to my character, but without them I wouldn't be what I am. You either accept me as I am or you don't. At Manchester they decided to accept me from the start and it's paid off. That's all.

CANTONA, 1994.

Just as I can bring happiness to people with my spontaneity, my instinctiveness, so there are always going to be dark shadows, black stains.

CANTONA, 1994.

He certainly deserves the captaincy (of France) as far as his talent is concerned, but I'm not sure about his cultural knowledge, which seems pretty basic to me.

CLAUDE SIMONET, president of the French Football Federation, 1994.

The talk among your fellow professionals is that you are steadily becoming a dirty, nasty bastard.

JOHN FASHANU, Aston Villa striker, in newspaper column, 1994.

When he couldn't have things his own way he just took his bat home. Real soldiers grab their tin helmet, their rifle and a spade. They know that, on occasions, they have to dig in and make the best of it. When he didn't like it, he went missing. Back home to his music, painting and poetry.

HOWARD WILKINSON, Leeds manager, defending his decision to sell Cantona a year on, 1994.

I was with the chairman when Leeds came on inquiring about Denis Irwin. I was shaking my head and picked up a note pad to write down 'Eric Cantona'. I'm not clear why. It must have been an inspired moment. Leeds came back on 15 minutes later to say it was a possibility and we tied up the deal the next day.

FERGUSON, 1995.

I still think Cantona will let you down at the highest level. I think he let Leeds down against Rangers, twice, and in the big games, against Inter Milan or whoever, Cantona will go missing. He's a cry baby when the going gets tough.

GEORGE GRAHAM, Arsenal manager, 1994.

I made a number of enquiries and everyone said the same thing: 'He's totally unsuitable for English football'. Needless to say, I acted on that information and turned him down.

HOWARD KENDALL, former Everton manager, on considering Cantona before he broke into English football, 1995.

L'Angleterre contra Cantona

L'EQUIPE headline, 1994.

I just yelled: 'Off you go Cantona – it's an early shower for you'.

MATTHEW SIMMONS, Crystal Palace fan, explaining what he had said to
provoke Cantona's 'kung-fu' assault, 1995.

He is a genius, but there's this other side of him. Maybe he needs someone to examine him, a psychiatrist or something.

CHRIS WADDLE, Sheffield Wednesday player after Cantona's attack
on the fan at Selhurst Park, 1995.

Pressure is no excuse. I would take any amount of personal abuse for £10,000 a week (Cantona's reputed salary).

SIR STANLEY MATTHEWS, after Cantona's assault on abusive fan, 1995.

I'd have cut his balls off.

BRIAN CLOUGH on the Selhurst Park affair, 1995.

My initial feeling was to let him go. I couldn't imagine him playing for the club again...My wife Cath said: 'You can't let him off. Never let it be said you put winning the championship above doing the right thing.'

FERGUSON, in A Year in the Life, 1995.

In leaping the barrier boots first, Eric Cantona attacked English football in its most sensitive spot. The British have succeeded in eliminating violence to the point where the hideous metal fences supposed to protect the players have disappeared from their grounds. How can they acknowledge that the hooligans are now on the pitch, threatening the public.

LE MONDE editorial, 1995.

We are no longer interested in his escapades, his pseudo-philosophical bragging, his crudeness and the state of his soul. He lives his life and we live ours. And we don't miss him.

LE PROVENCAL newspaper, France, 1995.

You are a high profile public figure with undoubted gifts. As such you are looked up to by many young people. For this reason, the only sentence that is appropriate is two weeks in prison.

JEAN PEACH, head of Croydon magistrates, sentencing Cantona, 1995.
The sentence was overturned on appeal.

He sat there and took it all, so mild-mannered. It's difficult to imagine the volcano lurking within.

FERGUSON, on Cantona's sentencing, 1995.

Given Cantona's intellectuality, perhaps the surest way to wind him up would be to challenge him on a philosophical basis. It may well turn out, in the fullness of time, that what (Matthew) Simmons actually shouted was: 'Eric! Your concept of individuality is grossly diluted! You fail to acknowledge the despair pendant upon the absurdity of the human predicament! Abandon your semi-consciousness! You're acquiescent and you know you are! Come and have a go if you think you're Sartrian enough!

GILES SMITH, *Independent on Sunday* columnist, 1995.

But Eric, what about Monsieur Hyde,
Your second half, who grows Les Fleurs du Mal,
Who shows his studs, his fangs and disdain,
Who gets sent off, then nearly sent inside,
For thumping jobsworths at the Mondiale?
Leave thuggery to thugs and use your brain.

SEAN O'BRIEN, poet, reading 'Cantona' on BBC2's *On the Line*, 1994.

There was a young thug from Marseille
Who was playing at Crystal Palais
When a yob in the crowd
Abused him out loud
And got cuisse de grenouille up his nez.

LIMERICK competition winner on *l'afffaire Cantona*, *Daily Telegraph*, 1995.

1966 was a great year for English football. Eric was born.

NIKE ADVERTISING SLOGAN, 1994.

1995 was a great year for English football. Eric was banned.

T-SHIRT SLOGAN, on sale at Manchester City, Leeds, Liverpool etc, 1995.

Eric is no longer a footballer, he is an issue. He is either loved or hated like a chart-topping teeny band.

JIMMY GREAVES, prophesying in *The Sun* that Cantona would not be able to return to English football, 1995.

He did something condemnable, but we are not his judges. The qualities we chose him for are still there: performance, popularity, charisma.

ADVERTISING AGENCY SPOKESMAN defending Cantona's continued razor contract, 1995.

We'll never forget that night at Selhurst Park (when you buried that amazing volley against Wimbledon). Welcome back, Eric, from everyone who loves football.

POSTER outside Old Trafford – paid for by fans – before Cantona's comeback game, 1995.

I've been punished for striking a goalkeeper. For spitting at supporters. For throwing my shirt at a referee. For calling my manager a bag of shit. I called those who judged a bunch of idiots. I thought I might have trouble finding a sponsor.

CANTONA, in Nike cinema advertisement, 1995.

I play with passion and fire. I have to accept this fire occasionally does harm. I know it does. I harm myself. I am aware of it, I'm aware of harming others. But I cannot be what I am without those other sides of my character...I have to correct the faults, but must remain true to myself.

CANTONA, near the end of an eight-month FA ban, 1995.

Nobody in the history of football has been punished as hard as Eric. But he has never said a word about it or complained.

FERGUSON, 1995.

He's not a tackler. I'm fed up of telling him that. He doesn't know how to do it and usually ends up with a booking. Forwards abroad aren't expected to tackle – they conserve themselves for scoring or creating.

FERGUSON, before Cantona's comeback, 1995.

He is so mild-mannered when the volcano is not erupting inside him, and very patient with the youngsters.

FERGUSON, 1995.

I would not change anything, nothing at all. I am not always pleased with myself, but that's the way I am.

CANTONA, 1995

He's been punished for his mistakes. Now it's someone else's turn.

ADVERTISEMENT for Cantona's comeback game v Liverpool, 1995.

Wasn't it good to see Eric Cantona back in action? Let's hope this time he remembers that kicking people in the teeth is the Tory government's job.

TONY BLAIR, Labour leader, in speech to party conference
at time of Cantona's return from his long suspension, 1995.

I looked the other day, in a Venetian church, at a painting by Carpaccio in which St George displays the body of the dragon he has overcome. A small football crowd stands around watching. A turbaned notable drops a glance at the snail-like creature on its lead, with a lance through its throat. 'There goes Cantona', I thought. 'He's like that poor beast.' But also, of course, like St George.

KARL MILLER, *London Quarterly*, 1995.

To the Red hordes Cantona is a soul-mate, for just like them he is often persecuted and misunderstood...Manchester United is a maverick club, and Eric Cantona is the ultimate maverick.

MANCHESTER UNITED MAGAZINE, 1995.

What I don't understand is how a Frenchman can be playing for Manchester United. He's not even from England. They employ him to play football for them, not to go round hitting people.

LORD DENNING, 1995.

TONY CASCARINO

When I first arrived at Marseille, Bernard Tapie (then the club's owner) said to me: 'I didn't like Lee Chapman. I didn't like Mark Hateley. I like players like Chris Waddle.' I thought, oh shit, what am I doing here?

CASCARINO, Republic of Ireland striker, on life in the
French Second Division, 1995.

SIR BOBBY CHARLTON

The Prince of Wales's visit is big news here but Mr Charlton was even bigger.

BRITISH EMBASSY SPOKESMAN in Morocco, 1995.

ANDY COLE

Every signing you make is a gamble. But look at Andy's goal record. Some people would pay £10m for that.

ALEX FERGUSON, Manchester United manager, after buying Cole
from Newcastle for £7m, 1995.

It always amazes me when people say 'all he can do is score goals'. It's the most famous quote in football.

FERGUSON, 1995.

JOHN COLLINS

I don't normally run 70 yards with the ball, never mind go round the keeper and score.

COLLINS, Celtic midfielder, after scoring for
Scotland v San Marino, 1995.

STAN COLLYMORE

Collymore may have deserted you but God never will.

SIGN outside St Saviour's Church, Nottingham, after Collymore's £8.5m
departure to Liverpool, 1995.

He was the sort of player you always had to talk to, to build up and get him in the right mood. If his mind was right, he was a world-beater. Other times he'd be out on the pitch wondering why we'd picked him.

MICHAEL HUGHES, Stafford Rangers secretary, 1995.

Every Monday he'd ask me to give him a good boot on the ankle so that he'd be injured for Tuesday's running.

DARREN REILLY, former Walsall reserve colleague, recalling the
British record-signing's past, 1995.

I'd been saying how he should play for England, then he went out there and he was f****** hopeless. He was like a limp lettuce running around. But I've seen him and I know he can do things nobody else can. Left foot, right foot – it doesn't matter to Stan.

BARRY FRY, Birmingham manager, recalling his time as
Collymore's manager at Southend, 1995.

I'm no angel but I think I'm misunderstood more than anything else. I'm a pretty interesting bloke.

COLLYMORE, 1995.

LIAM DAISH

He'd jump up and head a jumbo jet away if it was threatening our goal.

BARRY FRY, Birmingham manager, on his centre-half and captain, 1995.

TONY DALEY

I get a lot of stick for my haircuts. But you'll always find that within a couple of weeks, there's a few kids have got them as well.

DALEY, Wolves winger renowned for exotic hairstyles, 1995.

If he could wear a designer outfit on the pitch and get away with it, he would.

MICHELLE DALEY, wife, 1995.

KENNY DALGLISH

He scored his few goals – not that many – but when he did, he shared his enjoyment with everybody. He had a better smile than Clark Gable. Beautiful teeth, arms wide...that's how he celebrated. He wasn't that big but he had a huge arse. It came down below his knees and that's where he got his strength from.

> BRIAN CLOUGH, in his *News of the World* column, 1995.

JULIAN DICKS

Hello, My Name is Satan

> SLOGAN on Dicks's favourite T-shirt, 1995.

All players in the Premiership have their names on their backs. This is supposedly for ease of identification but if anything it has created more confusion. Rumour has it that when Julian Dicks moved to Liverpool, he picked up the No 23 shirt because it said Fowler on it.

> KEVIN BALDWIN, author, *This Supporting Life: How To Be A Real Fan*, 1995.

I didn't have one bit of support from anybody at the club, either on the staff or up above me. Everybody said: 'What are you bringing him back for?'

> HARRY REDKNAPP, West Ham manager, recalling lukewarm attitude to his re-signing Dicks after the full-back's ninth sending-off, 1995.

JOSE DOMINGUEZ

I love him, the crowd loves him, everybody loves him. But when you analyse what he does, his final ball is crap. Full stop.

> BARRY FRY, Birmingham manager, on his Portuguese winger, later sold to Sporting Lisbon for £1m-plus, 1994.

IAIN DOWIE

REPORTER: Does Dowie score many goals in the air then?
HARRY REDKNAPP: Judging by the shape of his face, he must have headed a lot of goals.

> EXCHANGE at press conference as Redknapp revealed his intention to re-sign Dowie from Southampton, 1995.

I'M NOT THE BRAINIEST PERSON. I AIN'T GOT NO O-
LEVELS, NOTHING. I DIDN'T GO BACK FOR MY RESULTS
BECAUSE ALL I EVER WANTED TO DO WAS PLAY FOOT-
BALL.

JULIAN DICKS, 1995.

ILIE DUMITRESCU

I don't remember him from the World Cup, but I'm sure he impressed me and will do a great job for Spurs.

> ALAN SUGAR, Tottenham chairman, on agreeing to pay £2.6m
> for the Romanian midfielder, 1994.

JOHN FASHANU

I've got a sore ear. He has certainly got a sore eye. And every time he hits you he says: 'Sorry, baby'.

> SHAUN TEALE, Aston Villa defender, on tangling with Fashanu
> before the latter joined Villa from Wimbledon, 1993.

When you throw your elbows out like that, you are going to hit somebody. He was not going up like that for his own protection.

> KEVIN MORAN, Blackburn defender, suffering a broken nose
> in collision with Fashanu's elbow, 1993.

When I saw my face, I felt like Elephant Man. This is not a normal injury. Fashanu was playing without due care and attention.

> GARY MABBUTT, Tottenham captain, after receiving a fractured skull
> from Fashanu's flying elbow, 1993.

I was not booked over the Mabbutt incident, and I will be playing in just the same style. I am a senior professional, and I've been in the game 17 years.

> FASHANU, 1993.

LES FERDINAND

I was talking to the referee all the time. I'm surprised I never got booked. I was talking to Les as well, saying: 'Is he a friend of yours? Does he look after your babies?'

> CLIFFORD HERCULES, Aylesbury striker, alleging preferential treatment
> for Ferdinand during FA Cup defeat at QPR, 1995.

The No 9s here are a bit special. You can't just give the shirt to anyone.

> KEVIN KEEGAN, Newcastle manager, on paying £6m
> to QPR for Ferdinand, 1995.

We've got Les up front, yet at times we were starving him. If you've got a monster up there, you must feed him.

KEEGAN, after an unsatisfactory friendly against Celtic, 1995.

DUNCAN FERGUSON

He's tall, he's skinny, he's going to Barlinnie.

CELTIC FANS' SONG about ex-Ranger, 1995.

I'm confident that if we can get him signed up we can successfully influence the other side of his character. I don't think he's a bad lad at all, it's just that things got on top of him in Scotland. Perhaps he was something of a marked man in Glasgow. I think it might do him good to get away from there. I don't think he's as bad as he's painted – he couldn't be.

JOE ROYLE, Everton manager, after inheriting Ferguson – and the assault charge against him – 1994.

The more it has gone on, the more there seems to have been a vendetta or witch-hunt for him – and the lad ends up in prison.

ROYLE on Ferguson's prison sentence for head-butting Raith Rovers' John McStay while on probation, 1995.

I would say to Fergie: 'You can't burn the candle at both ends'. I tried to, but the trouble was that the candle was as long as Sauchiehall Street. He should stick to looking after his pigeons and avoid the bookies. The only advice I ever had about money was from turf accountants.

JIM BAXTER, former Scotland and Rangers player, 1993.

I still hope his talent won't be wasted but the danger lies off the field. I'm not sure he's grown up and learned to turn the other cheek. It should have happened long before now and I honestly believed it would. My worry is that in 10 years' time he'll look back and realise he was given good advice, but it'll be too late because his career will be over. I hope I'm wrong.

JIM McLEAN, his former manager at Dundee United, 1995.

I can drink like a chimney.

FERGUSON, quoted by former Rangers team-mate John Brown, *Blue Grit*, 1995.

He was breathalysed the night before his first derby, then went on to score a vital goal in the game. Roy of the Rovers stuff.

ROYLE, 1995.

He could be the biggest thing here since Dixie Dean.

ROYLE on the £4m striker's impact at Goodison, 1995.

Birdman of Barlinnie.

VARIOUS newspapers and magazines during the pigeon-fancying Ferguson's imprisonment for assaulting McStay, 1995.

He spent his first few days (in jail) working in D Hall, mopping up and cleaning out the toilet blocks. But he was skint and had to get a £2.50 advance on his first week's wage.

DEREK SHEARER, fellow inmate at Barlinnie, 1995.

TV just asked permission to interview Dunc and I said yes, but don't hold your breath. I'm just glad the referees can't understand what he's saying to them.

ROYLE, 1995.

KEVIN FRANCIS

Kev is unique and he'll get criticised from now until Domesday. Everywhere we go he gets called a donkey but, if that's the case, he's the most valuable donkey in the world.

DANNY BERGARA, Stockport manager, 1994.

To be fair, he had quite a nice touch on the ball. He was quite daunting. If ever I need any guttering fixing, I'll give him a call.

RAY WILKINS, QPR midfielder, after the Stockport striker had undone his team in FA Cup tie, 1994.

People point at me and say: 'Look at the size of him'. I feel like saying to them: 'What planet have you landed from? Haven't you ever seen a tall bloke before?'

FRANCIS, after his £800,000 move to Birmingham, 1996.

Paul Gascoigne

He's matured a lot. We wouldn't have signed him if we thought he wasn't right. If he farts in front of the Queen, we get blemished.

PAUL McGAUGHEY, Adidas business unit manager,
on their sponsorship deal with Gascoigne, 1995.

He's an intelligent boy who likes to let people think he's stupid. He doesn't have a bad bone in his body but he does some stupid, ridiculous things. That's what makes him so interesting.

ALLY McCOIST, Rangers striker, 1996.

There's no nastiness in him. He just might say the wrong thing, or burp at the wrong time. He'll realise his mistake, but it's too late.

TERRY VENABLES, England coach, 1994.

Gascoigne came on and the team lost its balance. Why? Because Gascoigne is an attacking player, he has imagination, he can be a saviour, he can see when team-mates aren't marked. But it is normal for Gazza that he is lacking in defensive phases.

ZDENEK ZEMAN, Lazio coach, after 0-0 draw with Cagliari, 1995.

Doubts about Gascoigne's fitness to last 90 minutes persist, and it has been suggested that Taylor might send him out to run the Poles ragged for 45 minutes. Only a twisted cynic would say that half an oaf is better than none.

DAVID LACEY, football correspondent, *The Guardian*, 1993.

Consider the list of sins: the unfunny funny faces, the 'Fog on the Tyne' and 'Geordie Boys' raps, having a best friend called Five Bellies – these lapses of taste alone should be enough to consign him to the cultural scrapheap somewhere between Paul Daniels and Black Lace. I mean, imagine for a second, Gazza, if he wasn't such an astonishing footballer, what an irritating twat he'd be; and if he wasn't a footballer at all, how easily he'd fit among the whiteshirts singing 'Get your tits out for the lads'. And yet he redeems it all with every ball borne across the grass on angels' wings.

DAVID BADDIEL, comedian, in *The Independent Magazine*, 1993.

I'm too big to be sacked. You can call me Chris Eubank, but that's the way I see it.

> GASCOIGNE towards end of his time with Lazio, 1995.

He will only return to Rome as a tourist.

> SERGIO GRAGNOTTI, Lazio president, 1995.

I left because it's not nice to stay where you're not wanted.

> GASCOIGNE on leaving Lazio, 1995.

Our shot-putters are in better condition than Gazza.

> LINFORD CHRISTIE, Olympic sprinter, 1993.

I think it's the lightest he's been since he was four.

> VENABLES, on a slimline Gazza, 1995

I've given up beer and guzzling. My only lapse is to have a few toffees.

> GASCOIGNE, by now with Rangers, 1995.

When I lost all the pounds they said I was too skinny. When I put it on I was too fat.

> GASCOIGNE, 1995.

Even then he was off his head, completely crackers. He would put sweets down his socks and then give them to teachers to eat.

> STEVE STONE, Nottingham Forest midfielder, on his former schoolmate and England colleague, 1995.

Sometimes when players are down they just go out and get drunk. I can't even do that because I get followed.

> GASCOIGNE on the pressures of life in the Glasgow 'goldfish bowl', 1995.

Oh well then, can I just have an each way on him making a complete prat of himself.

> PUNTER in newspaper cartoon after bookies stopped taking bets on Gascoigne being sent off in his first Rangers v Celtic game, 1995.

They asked me things like: 'How big are Gazza's balls?'

VINNIE JONES, Wimbledon midfielder, on going to speak
to the boys of Eton College, 1996.

Tyneside's very own Renaissance man. A man capable of breaking both leg and wind at the same time.

JIMMY GREAVES, 1996.

RYAN GIGGS

I admire his pace and skills. I'd only look that fast if you stuck me in the 1958 FA Cup final.

RICK HOLDEN, Manchester City winger, 1993.

He's been playing crap since he met me.

DANI BEHR, TV presenter during her time as Giggs's girlfriend, 1994.

Giggs was a big problem for us all evening, but the biggest problem is that he does not have a German passport.

BERTI VOGTS, Germany coach, after his
team's victory over Wales, 1995.

I said before the game that we would win, but your talent overwhelmed my mind.

URI GELLER, spoon-bending psychic and Reading fan, to Giggs
after Manchester United's FA Cup win at Elm Park, 1996.

DAVID GINOLA

I didn't buy him to change him. He gives you things I couldn't find in England. That's the only reason you should buy foreign players. You haven't seen anyone in English football like him. He goes past good players.

KEVIN KEEGAN, Newcastle manager, on his signing from
Paris St-Germain, 1995.

FROG ON THE TYNE

DAILY STAR headline, 1995.

I wanted Ginola. I was desperate to get him. I thought he was fantastic. But as soon as I realised he was on £500,000 a-year net I knew I had no chance. As soon as I was told (his salary), I crossed him off – there was no way Arsenal were going to pay £800,000 or more. But he must be getting it now.

GEORGE GRAHAM, former Arsenal manager, *The Glory and the Grief*, 1995.

Men should love his skills and women his looks...He could end up being popular enough to replace Robbie in Take That.

CHRIS WADDLE, Sheffield Wednesday and former Marseille
midfielder, 1995.

He has pace, trickery and vision. You are not supposed to have all three.

KEEGAN, 1995

Both macho and new man. You couldn't find a better model.

COLIN WOODHEAD, Cerruti spokesman, on Ginola's other occupation, 1996.

I've heard Ginola say on TV that English people could not understand him being left out. Well, I'm not here to please the English.

AIME JACQUET, France coach, 1995.

I'm told he ran up the tunnel and dived in the bath.

JOE ROYLE, Everton manager, suggesting Ginola dives, 1995.

KEITH GILLESPIE

Keith took to school a bit later than many kids. There was a time when he'd rather watch *The Muppet Show*.

HARRY GILLESPIE, father of the Northern Ireland winger, 1995.

It staggers me that someone who is expected to play football at the highest level can carry on the way he does. There are often women back at the house and sometimes they're making a noise at four in the morning.

DAVID WOOD, university lecturer and Gillespie's neighbour,
on the Newcastle winger's penchant for partying in quiet Tyneside suburb, 1995.

BRUCE GROBBELAAR

I'd rather have Bruce Grobbelaar trying to throw a game than Dave Beasant trying to win one.

SOUTHAMPTON fan on *Six-O-Six* radio phone-in at the time of Grobbelaar's arrest on match-fixing charges, 1994.

He's so strong under pressure I call him Crocodile Dundee – or Indiana Jones when he wears that bush hat of his.

LAWRIE McMENEMY, Southampton director of football, 1995.

I've always said there were road sweepers and violinists who make up a football team. Bruce is a lead violinist.

McMENEMY, signing Grobbelaar from Liverpool, 1994.

RUUD GULLIT

He's here on a bus ride. He will just go around, see the sights and say 'thanks very much'.

VINNIE JONES on the Dutchman's arrival at Chelsea, 1995.

For ageing foreigners, our league must look like a global lottery. It's You – and a giant finger teases the dreadlocks of Ruud Gullit. Yes I know he was one of the world's greatest players. But 'was' is a very significant word in football.

JIMMY GREAVES in his *Sun* column before Gullit had played for Chelsea, 1995.

It was like watching an 18-year-old playing in a game for 12-year-olds.

GLENN HODDLE, Chelsea manager, on Gullit's debut v Everton, 1995.

He can still destroy you with one pass.

JOE JORDAN, Bristol City manager, after Gullit made one of his early Chelsea appearances at Bristol in a friendly, 1995.

The Rolls Royce of Rastafarians.

DAILY MIRROR, 1995.

My pot-bellied pigs don't squeal as much as him.

JONES, after being sent off for fouling Gullit, 1995.

WHAT CAN'T I DO NOW THAT I COULD NOT DO SEVEN YEARS AGO? I CAN'T
BE A GOALKEEPER.

RUUD GULLIT after first game for Chelsea, 1995.

He knows far too much about football. We're not having him on again.

ANDY GRAY, Sky commentator and former Scotland striker,
after Gullit's erudite analysis of a match 1996.

GHEORGHE HAGI

He's got a great left foot. He could open a can of beans with that foot.

RAY CLEMENCE, former England goalkeeper and radio summariser
on the Romanian midfielder, World Cup, 1994.

That Hagi's got a left foot like Brian Lara's bat.

DON HOWE, England coach and ITV pundit, World Cup finals, 1994.

He's a lazy sod, but he can't half play.

TERRY YORATH, Wales manager, after Hagi had destroyed his team, 1993.

ALAN HANSEN

I never liked pundits before I became one.

HANSEN, *Match of the Day* analyst, 1995.

He looks like a pissed vampire.

CHRIS DONALD, editor, *Viz* magazine, 1994.

RENE HIGUITA

I've never seen anything like it. He must have given his last three managers heart attacks.

TERRY VENABLES, England coach, on the Colombian goalkeeper's
'scorpion' save, Wembley, 1995.

We've got absolutely no interest in him. We've got a keeper with a better trick – he stops the ball with his hands.

RON ATKINSON, Coventry manager, after Higuita's acrobatics, 1995.

What's wrong with a simple catch? If he'd done that playing for England, Jack Charlton would have punched him on the nose and it would have been his last cap.

GORDON BANKS, England World Cup-winning goalkeeper, 1995.

MATTY HOLMES

Matty drives a sponsored Lada and used to get absolutely slaughtered by the lads. But he won't care – he'll park that Lada alongside the flashier motors in the Blackburn players' car park without batting an eyelid.

STEVE POTTS, West Ham defender, on Holmes's
transfer to Blackburn, 1995

MARK HUGHES

The centre-forward with the on-pitch disposition of something let loose on the streets of Pamplona.

JIM WHITE, author, *Are You Watching, Liverpool?*, 1994.

It reminded us who we were.

PAUL INCE, Manchester United midfielder, on Hughes' equaliser
in the dying seconds of the FA Cup semi-final, 1994.

A warrior you could trust with your life.

ALEX FERGUSON in David Meek and Mark Hughes,
Hughsie, The Red Dragon, 1994.

TERRY HURLOCK

He came in to me at Millwall with his leg high and whacked me in the chest. As I fell, I flicked out at him and caught him. All the lads rushed in and it really kicked off. Best thing was, he got sent off and I didn't even get booked. Marvellous.

IWAN ROBERTS, Leicester striker, 1995.

PAUL INCE

At Manchester, everyone called me Guv. I hope it'll be the same here.

INCE, arriving for training at Inter Milan after leaving United, 1995.

Paul Ince wants everyone to call him Guvnor, but we call him Incey.

LEE SHARPE, United colleague, 1995.

The Sunday after the FA Cup final, I heard that Ince was going around saying it was to be his last game for United. Then, on the Monday, there's Inter on the bloody phone. It's too much of a coincidence.

ALEX FERGUSON, United manager, 1995.

The man of a thousand faces, all of them snarling.

JIMMY GREAVES in *The Sun*, 1995.

L'asino della Settimana (Donkey of the Week).

GUERIN SPORTIVO magazine, Italy, 1995.

DENIS IRWIN

You don't get many of those for nothing, I can tell you.

WILLIE DONACHIE, Everton coach, recalling how he and Joe Royle
picked up the Manchester United full-back on a free transfer
from Leeds for Oldham, 1995.

DAVID JAMES

Armani's No 1!

KOP chant after the Liverpool goalkeeper began modelling, 1996.

An extraordinary looking man – and an important player for Liverpool.

GIORGIO ARMANI, designer, explaining why he chose James as a model, 1996.

VINNIE JONES

Well, stone me. We've had cocaine, bribery and Arsenal scoring two goals at home. But just when you thought there truly were no surprises left in football, Vinnie Jones turns out to be an international player.

JIMMY GREAVES, *Sun* columnist, 1995.

I've already been on the phone to my mate who does all my tatoos and told him to start practising the Welsh dragon.

JONES, Wimbledon midfielder, on his call-up by Wales, 1994.

I want to become the most tatooed footballer in Britain. That way I'd know I've had a successful career.

JONES, in *Vinnie: A Kick in the Grass*, 1995.

I don't have to prove anything, but I know I can hold my head up as an international player now. I just kept screaming at them, winding them up, and in the end they were running out of ideas.

JONES on his contribution to Wales' 1-1 draw with Germany, 1995.

The weather's great, I'm barbecued up, the animals are well and the season is here. That's when I shoot myself in the foot every time.

JONES, looking forward to a fresh campaign, 1995.

The mistake I made was not getting the hell out of the hotel bar about two hours earlier than I did and going straight to bed.

JONES, on reports that he bit a journalist's nose in a Dublin bar, 1995.

The world would be a better place if some of the kids that came out of there (Eton College) had half the bollocks Vinnie's got.

JOE KINNEAR, Wimbledon manager, on Jones's coaching engagement at Eton College, 1995.

Vinnie Jones does not deserve to be considered a footballer. Getting kicked is part of the job in France as well as in England, but the real scandal is that someone like Jones gets to be a star, to make videos and become an example for kids.

DAVID GINOLA, Newcastle's French winger, 1995.

I like the telly side of things. I'd like to be the young, or the new, Wogan.

JONES on his ambitions for life after football, 1995.

We'd love him to do our cookery, gardening and arts and crafts presenting. We think he'd be very good.

CHANNEL 4 SPOKESMAN after Jones's 'new Wogan' admission, 1995.

Orwell said that political speech was the defence of the indefensible. Michael Heseltine is the Vinnie Jones of the indefensible.

ALLISON PEARSON, television reviewer, *The Observer*, 1995.

I'm still on the transfer list but Alex Ferguson has yet to take the hint.

JONES, 1996

I really think I've got a lot to offer the game as far as being a manager is concerned.

JONES, 1996.

JUNINHO

He's not getting a club car – he's getting a snowplough.

BRYAN ROBSON, Middlesbrough player-manager, to reporters who wondered whether the Brazilian would be able to cope with the cold in the North-east, 1995.

He can control and pass, he's got a quick mind, he's small, he's Brazilian...

HOWARD WILKINSON, Leeds manager, after Juninho's Premiership debut, 1995.

He's tiny. I half expected him to go out with a school satchel on his back. If he had, I would have trod on his packed lunch.

ANDY THORN, Wimbledon defender, 1995.

They didn't hurt me. It's no different to Brazil. I am small, but I am tough.

JUNINHO on a torrid reception by Leeds' defenders on his debut, 1995.

What the scouts' reports said about the Brazilian boy frightened me to death. So I threw 'em in the bin.

BARRY FRY, Birmingham manager, after beating Middlesbrough in Coca-Cola Cup, 1995.

ANDREI KANCHELSKIS

When he was playing in Russia he was earning £2 a month. Last year we paid him £350,000. What does he want?

ALEX FERGUSON on Andrei Kanchelskis's transfer request, 1995.

ROY KEANE

Nicknamed Damien, after the character in *The Omen*. He's mad but he's funny too.

RYAN GIGGS, Manchester United team-mate, 1994.

I'm only just good enough for Manchester United. If I go to Italy it will only be for a holiday.

KEANE on speculation linking him with *Serie A* clubs, 1994.

The most victimised player in the game. He only needs to make one tackle and he's booked.

ALEX FERGUSON, Manchester United manager, 1996.

GARY KELLY

I've never seen a better full-back in my life.

JACK CHARLTON, Republic of Ireland manager, on the Leeds right-back, 1995.

GEORGI KINKLADZE

Please not to call me Russian.

KINKLADZE, Georgian international, on joining Manchester City, 1995.

It's a pity he isn't English. There again, he probably wouldn't get picked anyway.

ALAN BALL, Manchester City manager and former champion of
Matthew Le Tissier's England claims, 1995.

JURGEN KLINSMANN

Me dive? Never. I always go straight for goal.

KLINSMANN, Germany striker, World Cup finals, 1994.

I was watching Germany and I got up to make a cup of tea. I bumped into the telly and Klinsmann fell over.

FRANK SKINNER, comedian, 1994.

It was only a couple of days before travelling to England that a friend of mine warned me that I was in a big trouble (because of his reputation for diving). He told me my only chance was to make a joke about it.

KLINSMANN, on the 'dive-in' by Tottenham players after his debut goal
at Sheffield Wednesday, 1994.

I was honestly surprised by this reputation as a diver. I ask people: 'Tell me a dive'. They say 'Milan versus Monaco last year'. But that was a horrible one. Costacurta left three stripes in my calf and had to be sent off immediately.

KLINSMANN, 1995.

OOH-AAH WUNDERBAR

SUN headline, 1994.

I admire the way he plays with a smile on his face. There are too many who look like they are having a bad day at the office. They show strain and stress, but Jurgen smiles his way through and that's why the fans have taken to him.

KEVIN KEEGAN, Newcastle manager, 1994.

One thing I do find about London is that I'm saying the same things all the time. Everyone asks for interviews and exclusives, but everything has been said about me that can be.

KLINSMANN, 1994.

I felt obliged to offer him my shirt, but he didn't want it.

PAUL FRANCE, Altrincham defender, on obtaining Klinsmann's shirt after FA Cup tie, 1995.

As a manager you shouldn't admire your players, but I have to say I admire Klinsmann. He's the perfect professional. Sometimes you think he must do something wrong but he is immaculate all the time. I was surprised when he left.

OSSIE ARDILES, Klinsmann's former manager at Tottenham, 1995.

Technically he is not a brilliant player, but he will always score because of his industry and persistence.

GUNTER NETZER, former West Germany playmaker, 1995.

Both Gerry Francis and I believed he would be staying another season. I now know he needed one year with us to relaunch his career. He wanted to hike up his price so he could go and get a fortune in Germany.

ALAN SUGAR, Tottenham chairman, the day Klinsmann announced he was moving to Bayern Munich, 1995.

I brought one of the world's greatest players here to fix a problem, but it created another one. It relaunched his career and attracted all those offers for him.

ALAN SUGAR, 1995

You take it and auction it for charity. I wouldn't wash my car with it.

SUGAR, on the autographed Spurs shirt with which Klinsmann
had presented him after his farewell game, 1995.

It wasn't a question of money. You could see that from his lifestyle. At the Tottenham training ground there was a rainbow of cars, Mercedes, BMWs, whatever, and there was Klinsmann's two-door Volkswagen.

ARDILES, 1995.

ALEXI LALAS

Lalas resembles the love child of Rasputin and Phyllis Diller.

SPORTS ILLUSTRATED magazine on the United States defender 1994.

His beard, it's getting longer than his hair.

KEVIN KEEGAN, ITV pundit, World Cup finals, 1994.

MATTHEW LE TISSIER

I'm told he watches videos. I wonder if he's seen *Matt Le Tissier Unbelievable*? Maybe I should send him one.

LE TISSIER, Southampton midfielder, on Terry Venables, England manager, 1995.

Brazil would pick Le Tiss

BANNER at England v Brazil match, Wembley, 1995.

So having put his pal in the firing line, how has Le Tiss repaid him? By disappearing off the face of the earth in just about every game so far.

JIMMY GREAVES, *Sun* columnist on suggestions that Dave Merrington
was made manager of Southampton because he had
Le Tissier's support, 1995.

The first time I saw him I thought: 'Lucky Bastard, he's chipped that pass 80 yards'. After the fourth time, I thought: 'Maybe he's not so lucky after all'. OK, he doesn't run about and bash people, but in a mediocre side he scores unbelievable goals and makes things happen.

BARRY FRY, Birmingham manager, 1995.

You are never sure you want him playing for you, but you are sure you do not want him playing against you.

DARIO GRADI, Crewe manager, before FA Cup tie at Southampton, 1996.

I am happy in my life and I love Southampton. Being happy is very important to me and I don't see why I should disrupt that for the sake of a couple of quid.

LE TISSIER, 1995.

Other players might have won more caps but they won't be able to tell anyone they were better players than me. Long after I pack the game up, I'll be able to tell my kids I was one of the best players in the Premiership. That might make me sound like a big-headed twerp, but it's true.

LE TISSIER, after again being left out of the England squad, 1995.

JASON LEE

The problem with him having that great lump on top of his head is that I'm not sure he knows at which angle the ball will come off. It takes him so long to put it up I'm often waiting around to give my team talk.

FRANK CLARK, Nottingham Forest manager,
on his striker's 'pineapple' hairstyle, 1995.

Jason became one of those awkward players that defenders found difficult to handle. Yet a couple of middle-class wide-boys on TV who know nothing have helped him become victimised.

CLARK after Frank Skinner and David Baddiel poked fun
at Lee's hair on *Fantasy Football*, 1996.

HE'S GOT A PINEAPPLE ON HIS HEAD...

SONG by opposing fans, which Jason Lee claimed
affected his form, 1996

ROBERT LEE

I told him Newcastle was nearer to London than Middlesbrough was, and he believed me.

KEVIN KEEGAN, Newcastle manager, on how he lured Londoner Lee
to Tyneside ahead of Teesside, 1995.

My Mum and Dad scoured through Teletext. It said 'Lee to join Arsenal'. We automatically rang Arsenal's Club call to see what it said. It went through all my career details. It was weird.

LEE, Newcastle midfielder, on a transfer-that-never-was, 1995.

ANDERS LIMPAR

He has not passed the ball to me all season, so it was quite something to be involved in the build-up for Paul Rideout's goal and to receive the ball from Anders.

MATT JACKSON, Everton defender, on his Swedish colleague's
part in the goal which won the FA Cup, 1995.

He can be a little nervous at times, but really I've seen nothing like him in my life. He is a genius in terms of sheer ability. So much of him reminds me of Michel Platini.

JOE ROYLE, Everton manager, 1995.

GARY LINEKER

After I've been in Japan for two days I start to get depressed and I want to go home. The people get on my nerves. I just want to say: 'Stop bowing, will you?' There's no decent food, the beer's dead expensive, there's no proper cigarettes, you can't get drugs and all the women are ugly. Everyone's too nice – no wonder Gary Lineker went there.

NOEL GALLAGHER, member of the rock group Oasis
and Manchester City fan, 1995.

He had no feel for the game, no passion, and that's why, now that he's retired, he's best keeping out of football.

VINNIE JONES, Wimbledon midfielder, 1994.

DIEGO MARADONA

His left foot is like a hand.

OSSIE ARDILES, former Argentina player, 1994.

It's a dream having Diego here. It is like going out with Kim Basinger. You have to make the most of the moment, you don't think how long it will last.

ROBERTO CRUZ, president of lowly Deportivo Mandiyu,
on signing Maradona, 1994.

Fifa cut off my legs just when I had the chance to prove to my daughters that I could play with 20-year-olds.

MARADONA on leaving World Cup finals after failing a drug test, 1994.

I'm upset by Fifa's stupidity. I consider ephedrine a medicine, and I take it every day to be at my best for my public.

LUCIANO PAVAROTTI, opera singer, on Maradona's ban, 1994.

When we played them in Argentina he adopted our younger players and spent hours signing autographs. That's the side people don't see. Anyway, after they beat us he took us night-clubbing and footed the drinks bill. That makes him OK in my book.

EDDIE THOMSON, Australia manager, after Maradona's
expulsion for drug abuse, 1994.

There's a little bug telling me 'you still can'.

MARADONA planning a comeback, 1995.

I turn 35 but feel like 18. This is like a dream. I hope God will give me the necessary strength to continue running like I have in each game.

MARADONA after helping Boca Juniors to four wins in five games, 1995.

I was, I am and I always will be a drug addict. A person who gets involved in drugs has to fight it every day.

MARADONA, joining the Argentinian government's
anti-drugs campaign, 1996.

SIR STANLEY MATTHEWS

I don't know if I was all that good. I never saw myself play, so how do I know?

SIR STAN on his 80th birthday, 1995.

I'm no hero. Doctors and nurses are heroes. Surgeons, people like that. We had a real hero born right here in Stoke-on-Trent – Reginald Mitchell, who designed the Spitfire. He saved Britain. Now that's what I call a hero.

SIR STAN, 1995

BRIAN MCCLAIR

Looking back on it, I think he was not really a bench player – he isn't the kind of player who's going to come on and ignite a game. His effectiveness is over the full 90 minutes.

ANDY ROXBURGH, former Scotland manager, 1995.

ALLY MCCOIST

He's Superman and Roy of the Rovers rolled into one. We call him Golden Bollocks.

JOHN ROBERTSON, Hearts striker and Scotland team-mate, 1995.

You're like dogshit in the penalty box. We don't know you're there until the damage is done.

JOHN HUGHES, Celtic defender, to McCoist, 1995.

I met Michael Jackson backstage at the Tokyo Dome in '93, but to be honest, meeting Ally McCoist was a bigger buzz.

ALAN McGEE, Creation Records label owner, 1995.

ROY MCDONOUGH

I'm not a maniac. I'm one of the most easy-going blokes in the world. My girlfriend says I'm a soft touch.

McDONOUGH, Canvey Island striker, on the 19 sendings-off of his professional career, 1995.

Roy's the most ill-disciplined and occasionally terrifying player I've ever known. He could eat Vinnie Jones for breakfast.

DAVE CUSACK, McDonough's former manager at Dagenham & Redbridge, 1995.

PAUL MCGRATH

For us, Paul is the fly in the ointment. If he was stable, steady, I wouldn't have such urgent need of Phil Babb. But it's always in the back of my mind that Paul might have more problems with his knees, or that he might not bloody turn up for the World Cup.

JACK CHARLTON, Republic of Ireland manager, 1994.

Paul's every bit as good as (Franco) Baresi. He seems to have a magnetic head – everything comes to him.

ANDY TOWNSEND, Republic of Ireland captain, 1994.

Paul is one of the all-time greats, someone to compare with Bobby Moore. He has always been a very intimidating player. I used to tell him: 'Just look your opponents in the face, smile at them, and you'll frighten them to death'.

CHARLTON, Republic of Ireland manager, 1995.

PAUL MERSON

You wonder who Merson or Arsenal know. The whole thing stinks. He should be kicked out of football. He must be laughing his head off.

TERRY DICKS MP, Conservative, on the decision not to prosecute the Arsenal and England midfielder over his confessions of drug-taking, 1995.

I'm going to Gamblers' Anonymous – that's my night out now. Now I've got a choice to make – either I go back to the booze and the gambling or I go the other way.

MERSON after admitting his various addictions, 1995.

Some of the players still think I will be able to have the odd drink eventually. David Platt has the *Sporting Life* at breakfast and probably can't work out why I don't sit with him until he has put it away. He'll catch on slowly, like most people do.

MERSON, 1995.

GARY NEVILLE

If he was an inch taller he'd be the best centre-half in Britain. His father is 6ft 2in – I'd check the milkman.

ALEX FERGUSON, Manchester United manager, on the 5ft 11in Neville, 1996.

We should all stop talking about Gary's height, take no notice and appreciate what he has got, which is a terrific temperament, character, composure, ability to read the game and organise.

DAVID SADLER, former United and England centre-half, 1996.

STEVE NICOL

Five million pounds and worth every penny. He could sit in an armchair and play, because he's got a brain.

DAVID PLEAT, Sheffield Wednesday manager, on signing the former Liverpool defender on a free transfer, 1995.

CARLTON PALMER

He never shuts up. Talks some rubbish, but we throw that away and sometimes some intelligence comes out.

GORDON STRACHAN on his new Leeds team-mate, 1994.

PAUL PARKER

Paul's foot is in plaster, so he has to wear a shoe-thing so he can walk. As his image is so important to him, he has managed to get eight shoe-things in different colours to co-ordinate with his various outfits. The trials and tribulations of a fashion slave...

BRIAN McCLAIR, Manchester United colleague, in his 'Life of Brian' column, *United Magazine*, 1995.

PAUL PESCHISOLIDO

Paul's kind of macho, so he never does the cooking or the housework.

KARREN BRADY, Birmingham MD and wife of the Stoke striker, in Elle magazine, 1995.

The English press have nicknamed us the Cindy Crawford and Richard Gere of football.

BRADY.

DAVID PLATT

Crewe to captain.

ADVERTISING slogan after Platt's elevation to England captaincy, 1994.

An extraordinarily intelligent player, 10 years ahead of his time.

GIANLUCA VIALLI, former Juventus team-mate, 1994.

GICA POPESCU

Popescu's a bloody moaner. If he had a cracked eyelash he wouldn't want to play...Gerry (Francis) and I just burst out laughing one day when he said, deadly serious: 'Someone tackled me on Saturday and my back hurts a little now. I don't think I can play the next game.'

ALAN SUGAR, Tottenham chairman, after selling the Romanian libero to Barcelona, 1995.

JAMIE REDKNAPP

He likes nothing better than to phone up the other players in their hotel rooms, making out he's from the press, and trying to get them to slag off our team-mates. He tried it on with me once, making out he was from *The Star*, but I sussed him out straight away.

STEVE HARKNESS, Liverpool defender, 1995.

PETER REID

He can't run, can barely breathe, his legs have gone all soft and can't kick a ball more than ten yards. Yet look what he does. He calms everyone down. It's just what we needed.

MICK WALKER, Notts County manager, 1994.

MARC RIEPER

We call him Superman. He's got the looks, he's really well educated and has everything going for him. We all hate him.

HARRY REDKNAPP, West Ham manager, on his Danish centre-back, 1995.

ROMARIO

God created me to delight people with my goals.

ROMARIO, 1994.

He's the only player I know who can dribble within a square metre.

JOHAN CRUYFF, Barcelona coach, 1994.

He's a player out of a cartoon strip.

JORGE VALDANO, Real Madrid manager, 1994.

Romario is arrogant, petty-minded and without his football he would be a criminal.

DELMA KATZ, mother of Romario's girlfriend, 1995.

NEIL RUDDOCK

I always make sure he's on my side in training. There's not an ounce of compromise in him.

IAN RUSH, Liverpool captain, 1994.

If Razor had hit me properly, I don't think I'd be here to talk about it.

ROBBIE FOWLER, Liverpool striker, after an alleged airport fracas with Ruddock following a trip to Russia, 1995.

I never saw the incident. I just saw a trail of blood going through the green customs exit. I don't think many people mess with Razor.

STAN COLLYMORE, Liverpool colleague, 1995.

People have got me all wrong really. Underneath I'm just a big softie really.

RUDDOCK, Liverpool defender, 1995.

PETER SCHMEICHEL

Probably the only playmaking goalkeeper in the country.

ALAN HODGKINSON, Manchester United goalkeeping coach, on the Dane's distributive prowess, 1995.

Peter returns, but the operation has not worked because he still won't admit it when he makes a mistake.

BRIAN McCLAIR, 'The Life of Brian', *United Magazine*, 1995.

I just went up the park to cause a bit of mayhem. There was nothing to lose.

SCHMEICHEL on his sortie upfield in the dying moments of the FA Cup Final, 1995.

One goal and suddenly he's a superstar.

ANDY COLE, United striker, after Schmeichel's goal v Rotor Volgograd, 1995.

LES SEALEY

He is the Mike Reid of football. He has had used car lots, travel agencies, pubs. He reminds me of Frank Butcher. He has the big gold chains, dodgy Rolex, big cigars – he's very impressionable. Half way through training he might walk out saying 'I've had enough of this' and go off to flog cars. The next day he'd turn up as if nothing had happened and you wouldn't be able to get a shot past him.

RAY HARFORD, Blackburn assistant manager, on his former Luton goalkeeper, 1994.

One day he announced he wanted to be known as 'The Cat'. We'd be playing a match and you'd hear 'The Cat's ball!' and Les would come for it. But he didn't always get there, so Mick Harford christened him 'Tiddles'.

STEVE FOSTER, former Luton team-mate, 1994.

The last thing you could say about Les is that he's a natural athlete.

NIGEL SPINK, Aston Villa goalkeeper, on his former colleague, 1994.

DAVID SEAMAN

Nay-eeeem from the halfway line, Nay-eeeem from the halfway line...

SPURS FANS' SONG after Nayim, an ex-Tottenham player, had scored from long range to beat Seaman and win the Cup-Winners' Cup for Zaragoza, 1995.

Q: Why is Nayim the most virile player in Europe?
A: Because he can lob Seaman from 50 yards.

SPURS' FANS' joke, 1995.

ALAN SHEARER

The best striker I've ever faced, without question – and that was only
in training.

DAVID MAY, Manchester United and former Blackburn defender, 1994.

Alan is old beyond his years, really, he's like 23 going on 50. His
favourite record is 'Sailing' by Rod Stewart. It makes me feel like slap-
ping him round the face and saying 'get a grip on yourself!'

GRAEME LE SAUX, Blackburn colleague, 1994.

He's a lad's lad. It's more important for him to be accepted by all the
lads than to receive all the accolades that have come his way.

MIKE NEWELL, Blackburn striking partner, 1995.

DAVIE SINCLAIR

He's so hard he's got tatoos on his teeth.

JIMMY NICHOLL, Raith Rovers manager, on his club's defender, 1995.

TREVOR SINCLAIR

He is so quick that on a winter's day I could play him in his overcoat and the opposition defenders still wouldn't be able to catch
him.

NEIL BAILEY, Blackpool youth team coach, recalling the QPR
forward's early days with the Lancashire club, 1995.

NEVILLE SOUTHALL

I wouldn't go so far as to say he's a complete nutcase, but he comes
very close to it.

TERRY YORATH, Wales manager, 1993.

I stayed with the Villa chairman (Doug Ellis) the night I signed. His wife even ironed my shirt, which I had to smile about after all the trouble at Palace (with chairman Ron Noades).

GARETH SOUTHGATE, 1996.

After Forest played Spurs I tried to get Jurgen Klinsmann's autograph. He didn't look up – he thought I was a fan – and I felt like shouting: 'Oi, I've just played against you!'

STEVE STONE, 1996.

When I walked through the door I had an open mind about him. I had seen one or two goals go in on the telly, and people were pointing fingers at the big man. We had a couple of days that were interesting between us. Things were crackling about a bit. He is nicely awkward, let's say, and is as strong-willed as anyone you will ever find.

JOE ROYLE, Everton manager, 1995.

GARETH SOUTHGATE

You're a better writer than a footballer.

VINNIE JONES, Wimbledon midfielder during derby v Crystal Palace, 1995.
Southgate had a column in the Croydon Advertiser.

GARY SPEED

If I was a skinhead Yorkshireman and had tattoos and went around kicking people I'd be all right.

SPEED, Leeds midfielder, on being barracked by his own fans, 1994.

STEVE STONE

My first reaction was that it was an incredible goal. But I've just heard he's saying that he just meant to cross the ball. Either way, he's ruined my weekend.

GERRY FRANCIS, Tottenham manager, after Stone's winner
for Nottingham Forest, 1995.

GORDON STRACHAN

There's nobody fitter at his age – except maybe Raquel Welch.

RON ATKINSON, Coventry manager, on Strachan's outstanding
form shortly after his 39th birthday, 1996.

ALAN STUBBS

They say he takes the odd chance at the back, which is a little like remembering Bobby Moore for the goal he gave away in Poland.

BRUCE RIOCH, Bolton manager, 1995.

CHRIS SUTTON

I first went to see the Blackburn chairman (Robert Coar) and we had a meal together in a hotel on Blackpool sea front. My first course was chilled melon. I remember it cost £1.85 and by the time I had finished they had agreed to pay up the £5m.

SUTTON, Blackburn striker, recalling move from Norwich, 1994.

That's a good deal for Blackburn because he's got a heart as big as his new wage packet.

IAN BUTTERWORTH, Norwich defender, 1994

MICKEY THOMAS

I'd have been better off signing Lord Lucan. But I still thought Mickey would turn up at Heathrow on Saturday night, probably on the back of Shergar.

LYN JONES, Inter Cardiff manager, after finding the former Welsh international was unable to travel abroad under the terms of his probation after a prison sentence, 1994.

It's a sham the Home Office won't let me go to Poland for the Uefa Cup game. As if I'd do a runner in Katowice.

THOMAS, 1994

CARLOS VALDERRAMA

Before I played against him I thought he was a bit lazy, a luxury player, but you try getting the ball off him. It took three of us at one point.

GRAEME LE SAUX, England defender, on the Colombian playmaker, 1995.

MARCO VAN BASTEN

Marco played football like a ballerina, like Nuryev with a colossal body, but eventually his ankle couldn't stand the strain.

RENE MARTI, the Swiss specialist who treated Van Basten before his retirement, 1995.

CHRIS WADDLE

For a defender, Chris running at you is the worst sight in football.

ALAN HANSEN, TV pundit and former Liverpool defender, 1993.

GEORGE WEAH

It's very hard for an African to make it in Europe. Look what happens when you get successful. People see a white man driving a Mercedes and assume he's a successful businessman. When they see a black man in a car like that, they think he's a drug dealer.

WEAH, Milan's Liberian striker, 1995.

BILLY WRIGHT

He was as good a bloke as he was a player. And he was a great player.

RON ATKINSON, Aston Villa manager and ITV summariser,
on the former England and Wolves captain's death, 1994.

IAN WRIGHT

How can Arsenal be boring when you watch players like Wright? I'd love him in my side.

HOWARD KENDALL, Everton manager, 1993.

Garbage Man of the Year

US SOCCER magazine award for 'bad-mouthing' American keeper
Tony Meola on his England debut, 1993.

The man is obviously a few sandwiches short of a picnic and it caused our club a lot of anxiety.

REG BURR, Millwall chairman, after the Arsenal striker
accused some Millwall fans of being racist, 1995.

I've seen other players get away with things that I'd never even contemplate, but people have this perception that I'm some kind of nutcase and I'm not like that at all.

WRIGHT, 1993.

Ian is not the sort of guy you can just go up to and say: 'Quieten down'.

BRUCE RIOCH, Arsenal manager, trying to sort out Wright's disciplinary problems, 1995.

TONY YEBOAH

His touch for the third was immaculate – it was in the net in the time it takes a snowflake to melt on a hot stove.

HOWARD WILKINSON, Leeds manager, on the Ghanaian's hat-trick v Ipswich, 1995.

Some players need a service once every 500 miles. Tony needs one about every 250,000. He comes in, trains, listens, contributes, practises, goes home, turns up for matches and does the business. A manager's dream.

WILKINSON, 1995.

He's like a combination of Gary Lineker and Mark Hughes. Very strong, good with his back to goal an excellent first touch. He knows where that 192 square feet of net is and normally hits it.

WILKINSON, 1995.

It's not his goals to games ratio, it's his goals to touches that impresses me.

JOE ROYLE, Everton manager, 1995.

Sometimes, when I score, I can't explain, even to myself, how I did it.

YEBOAH, 1995.

People say you can't turn yourself on and off like a tap. I believed that until I met Tony. He only comes alive during a match. The rest of the time he's so laid back you couldn't possibly guess what he's capable of.

JOHN PEMBERTON, Leeds defender, 1995.

Tony the Tiger Swears By Yorkshire Puds!

NORDALE FOODS' slogan after tabloid story about Yeboah's passion for Yorkshire pudding, 1995. (He later confirmed that he had actually eaten it only once.)

Clubs and Teams

AJAX

Ajax are not just the team of the Nineties, they are approaching football Utopia. Their concept of the game is exquisite, yet they have a physical superiority as well. They are Beauty and the Beast.

JORGE VALDANO, Real Madrid coach, 1995.

My system is very demanding. If one or two players are off-form, we become beatable. But when it works like it did here, I believe these 11 individuals become the perfect team.

LOUIS VAN GAAL, Ajax coach, after 2-0 away victory over Real Madrid, 1995.

They're like an eagle, with their wings spread wide as they glide menacingly forward.

ANDY ROXBURGH, technical adviser to Uefa, 1995.

It's amazing that they're the best club team in the world, and yet no one copies them. Yet it can be done. The intelligence comes from the coach, like a teacher at school. If you reach for perfection you get excellence. If you aim for half, you don't even get that.

TERRY VENABLES, England coach, 1996.

From the moment Ajax's players ran on to the pitch you could see they knew they were going to win.

ARTUR JORGE, Switzerland manager, after seeing the European Cup holders win in Dortmund, 1996.

ARSENAL

It doesn't bother me that we're not well liked. It's part of our history.

GEORGE GRAHAM, Arsenal manager, 1994.

I think we're criticised unfairly. Who else from the south has won the championship? People down here should give us a fair crack of the whip. We'll have a go. We'll go up north and take them on. Who else will?

GRAHAM, 1994.

AUXERRE

If one of our forwards had gone off on a stretcher, Auxerre would probably have sent somebody with him.

STEWART HOUSTON, Arsenal acting manager, 1995.

BARNSLEY

If they keep on playing like this, they'll end up playing for Chorley. And that's no disrespect to Chorley.

DANNY WILSON, Barnsley manager, after 5-0 hammering by Birmingham, 1995.

BILLINGHAM SYNTHONIA

Billingham Synthonia have the unique distinction of being the only club in Britain named after a fertiliser (though several other possible candidates immediately spring to mind).

HARRY PEARSON, author, *The Far Corner: A Mazy Dribble Through North-East Football*, 1994.

BIRMINGHAM CITY

Q: What attracted you to Birmingham City?
A: Nothing. I was told by my boss to come here.

KARREN BRADY, managing director, in interview with King's Heath Concorde FC fanzine, 1993.

From the Stadium of Light to the edge of darkness.

ANDY COLQUHOUN, *Birmingham Post*, quoting fan's comment on Jose Dominguez's move from Benfica to Birmingham, 1994.

I would expect all 72 of Barry Fry's players for £2m.

JOE KINNEAR, Wimbledon manager, denying he had bid £2m for Liam Daish, 1995.

BLACKBURN ROVERS

I feel there's something vulgar about the way Blackburn have spent millions to win the title.

JOHN MADEJSKI, Reading chairman and multi-millionaire, 1995.

BATTY AND LE SAUX THERE…ARGUING OVER WHO
HAS THE SILLIEST NAME.

RORY BREMNER as Desmond Lynam, Channel 4, 1995.

They have very talented players who are prepared to work their socks off for the good of the team. I keep reading about people not liking the way they play but I don't know any other way. Chris Sutton got more tackles in on David Phillips, who is our hub, than any other player this season, and if you've got a £5m front man who's prepared to do that, you've got a chance.

FRANK CLARK, Nottingham Forest manager, during Rovers' run
to the Premiership title, 1995.

We've got there a year early. We had planned to win it (the championship) next year so I suppose we had better go out and do it again.

JACK WALKER, Blackburn president and multi-millionaire benefactor, 1995.

You may have just caught a chorus of us in the dressing-room, singing: 'I'm forever blowing bubbles...'

GRAEME LE SAUX, Blackburn defender, on winning the
championship thanks to West Ham's draw with
Manchester United, 1995.

Before this match I told my players that they will be playing against 11 men ready to fight for each other for 90 minutes. I didn't expect them to be fighting with each other.

OLEG ROMANTSEV, Moscow Spartak coach, after altercation between
Graeme Le Saux and David Batty, Champions League match, 1995.

I'm not saying the dream is over. I'm not saying they won't win a trophy this season. But I am absolutely staggered that they haven't made more use of Jack Walker's money, that they didn't strike while the iron was at its hottest.

KEEGAN, Newcastle manager, after Blackburn's poor start
to the defence of their title, 1995.

BRAZIL

Brazil – You made me cry in 82, 86, 90. This time make me dance and I can die in peace.

BANNER at World Cup finals, 1994.

WE TRY TO PLAY GOOD FOOTBALL AND WIN MATCHES — IN THAT ORDER. THE ALTERNATIVE IS TO TRY TO WIN MATCHES AND HOPE THE FOOTBALL WILL FOLLOW. I SUPPOSE THAT IS WHAT BLACKBURN ARE DOING.

KEVIN KEEGAN, Newcastle manager, on Blackburn's pursuit of the title, 1995.

Bebeto was going at 100mph. These guys are dribbling maniacs.

ALEXI LALAS, United States defender, after defeat by Brazil,
World Cup finals, 1994.

The team of 1970 played with good organisation. When people speak of the great scorers we had them – Pele, Jairzinho, Rivelino, Tostao – they forget that it was also the team that allowed fewest goals in the competition. Do they expect Brazil to win the World Cup disorganised? We have a flat back four, zonal marking and possession of the ball. With that the players can be themselves. They can be Brazilians.

CARLOS ALBERTO PARREIRA, Brazil coach, 1994.

BRUGES

Even Poirot would struggle to find evidence that Bruges are a good side.

GARY LINEKER, Radio 5 Live pundit, 1995.

BULGARIA

What you have done for Bulgaria is much more than all Bulgarian diplomats and politicians have during this century.

PRESIDENT ZHELYU ZHELEV, welcoming the World Cup
semi-finalists back to Sofia, 1994.

CARLISLE UNITED

We can be bigger than Blackburn.

MICHAEL KNIGHTON, Carlisle chairman, 1995.

We have a 10-year plan to get into the Premiership, and now we are ahead of schedule.

KNIGHTON, celebrating the Third Division championship, 1995.
They were relegated a year later

CELTIC

There's nothing worse than sitting in the dressing-room at Celtic Park after a defeat, not a word being said, listening to them next door going mental.

ALLY McCOIST, Rangers striker, 1996.

It (winning the European Cup) might have been for Scotland, but it definitely wasn't for Britain. It was for Celtic.

> BILLY McNEILL, captain of the 1967 'Lisbon Lions', 1995.

We've got 26,000 seats with a better view than the referee's.

> FERGUS McCANN, Celtic owner, on the club's new stand, 1996

CHELSEA

Ken Bates paid £1 for Chelsea. He was done. Have you seen the way they are playing at the moment?

> BARRY HEARN, Leyton Orient chairman, 1995.

Stuff the team! They are the ones who got Chelsea in a mess in the first place. Chelsea have two great players – the boss and a Dutchman with worse knees than mine. I'd be waiting at the door with cards and a taxi for the rest of them – Dennis Wise excepted, for obvious reasons.

> JIMMY GREAVES on reports that the team supported Matthew Harding in his boardroom feud with chairman Ken Bates, November 1995.

COVENTRY CITY

I've been racing Formula One in a Mini Metro.

> BOBBY GOULD explaining why he had resigned as manager, 1995.

More divots than Gleneagles.

> GLENN HODDLE, Chelsea manager, after defeat at Highfield Road, 1996.

COWDENBEATH

Why the nickname 'Blue Brazil?' Easy. Cowden play in blue and have the same debt as a Third World country.

> BIG BOB, Cowdenbeath diehard, quoted in Ronald Ferguson,
> *Black Diamonds and the Blue Brazil*, 1993.

DONCASTER BELLES

Some of them came over like lager louts. I kept wondering how they could be so unprofessional.

> GILL WYLIE, Arsenal captain, on their rivals' performance
> on a TV documentary, 1995.

ENGLAND

England didn't create any more chances than Malta or Luxembourg did here.

EGIL OLSEN, Norway coach, after 0-0 draw in Oslo, 1995.

England can't always win 6-0. Bobby Charlton has retired.

DAVE BASSETT, Sheffield United manager, after another 0-0 draw, 1995.

EVERTON

We think we are a pub team, that's the way our mentality is – we will go anywhere and give anybody a game. We went into the Final with the pub team attitude that it doesn't matter who we play, we are going to have a right good go.

NEVILLE SOUTHALL, goalkeeper, after FA Cup final win over Manchester United, 1995.

The Dogs of War business has been laid to rest. We are in the Crufts class now.

JOE ROYLE, manager, after the final.

If anyone ever mentions the Everton School of Soccer Science to me again, well I'm sorry, I just don't see it.

ROY EVANS, Liverpool manager, after acrimonious derby draw, 1995.

Although I knew Everton I wasn't prepared for how big it is. Just dealing with the media is an experience – if we had one reporter at Oldham it constituted a press conference.

ROYLE, 1994.

GRIMSBY TOWN

There are goals to pursue here, just as there were at Juventus. They are simply smaller goals.

IVANO BONETTI, Grimsby's Italian forward, 1995.

the protests bothered me, would I not be hiding in a bunker?' Robert Chase on
...monstrations (above) against his chairmanship of Norwich

...ust yelled: 'Off you go Cantona – it's an early shower for you.' Matthew Simmons' version of
...nat provoked the Frenchman's leap into infamy (below).

'I was told I had a reputation in England for diving and my only chance was to make a joke out it.' Jurgen Klinsmann explaining his debut-goal dramatics for Spurs (above)

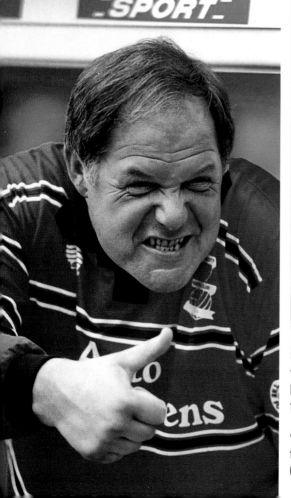

'An intelligent boy who likes to let people think he's stupid,' Ally McCoist on Gazza (above), the flawed flautist of Glasgow

'A management style based on the chaos theory.' Wolves' Mark McGhee hails Barry Fry (left)

'I've been a local government officer for 20 years and it gets easier. Refereeing is getting harder.' Stephen Lodge feels the pressure of the Premiership

'He's from Latin America – that's the way they are.' Kevin Keegan on Faustino Asprilla (striped shirt) after his fracas with Keith Curle (centre)

'Some of the players still think I'll b[e] able to have the odd drink eventually.' Paul Merson, pictured (left) pretending to be on the booz[e] before his admission of alcoholism

'Sometimes, when I score, I can't explain how I did it, even to myself[.]' Tony Yeboah (below) on the goalscorer's instinct

'Nice to see them together... don't know whether they were holding hands or not.' Glenn Hoddle on a ceasefire between feuding Chelsea directors Ken Bates (beard) and Matthew Harding

er all this is not a game for little ladies.' Arsenal's Rebecca Lonergan (foreground) and Karen
·ke of Liverpool do their best to disprove the theory of Placido Domingo

'The Divine Pony Tail.' Italian fans' banner in praise of Roberto Baggio (left)

'Brazil – you made me cry in 82, 86, 90. This time make me dance and I can die in peace.' Banner at World Cup final, 1994. *Below:* Brazil parade their trophy and the samba starts

beard's getting longer than his hair.' Kevin Keegan on USA defender Alexi Lalas (right)

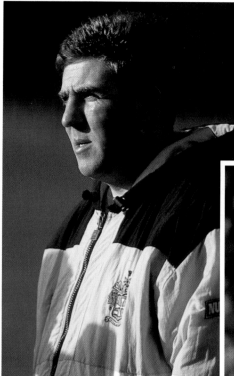

'He's fat, he's round, he's taken Leicester down.' Reading fans tease ex-manager Mark McGhee (left), who agreed he was overweight

'He was breathalysed before his first derby, then scored a vital goal.' Joe Royle on Everton's troubled talisman Duncan Ferguson (below)

We regard Millwall as the pinnacle of our careers.' Russia's Sergei Yuran (below, left) at start of ill-starred sojourn in south London with Vassili Kulkov

ITALY

On the pitch the Italians look no different to us. It was like playing Bournemouth on a wet Saturday.

> JASON McATEER, Republic of Ireland midfielder, after victory over Italy,
> World Cup finals, 1994.

LEEDS UNITED

We are like UNICEF at the moment, everyone is feeding off us. The ones who really get to me are the ex-players who are out of work and jump into the media to have a go at us.

> HOWARD WILKINSON, manager, responding to criticism, 1994.

I think this is the most wonderful place in Europe.

> TONY YEBOAH, Leeds' Ghanaian striker, 1995.

LEYTON ORIENT

Our aim is to kick shit out of everyone in the Third Division.

> BARRY HEARN, chairman, 1995.

It was disgusting. How dare the chairman of the club say something as irresponsible as that. Anyway, if we kicked shit, we wouldn't kick it straight.

> ORIENT SEASON TICKET HOLDER on Hearn's statement, 1995.

LIBERIA

The worst team to feature a European Footballer of the Year since George Best turned out for Dunstable Town.

> ANDY LYONS, editor, *When Saturday Comes* magazine, on George Weah's
> unhappy experience at the African Nations Cup, 1996.

LIVERPOOL

I think we have got to the stage where we are passing it for passing's sake, not for the end product. In the end you can pass yourself to sleep.

> ROY EVANS, manager, after defeat by Newcastle, 1995.

The gaffer sent me to see if I could spot a weakness and I found one. The half-time tea's too milky.

> KEVIN SUMMERFIELD, Shrewsbury coach, after watching his club's
> next FA Cup opponents crush Leeds 5-0 at Anfield, 1996.

MANCHESTER CITY

1976 was a strange year for English football – City won a trophy.

> T-SHIRT SLOGAN outside Old Trafford, 1995.

Manchester City is talked about as a big club. But it is not. It's a big club in image, it's got a big ground but its income is very low. Unless we raise that we cannot match our image.

> FRANCIS LEE, City chairman, 1995.

We are now on the right footing. The infrastructure of the club is in place. But a lot depends what happens on the field.

> LEE, 1995.

It's a bigger job than I thought in every aspect. It's a big stage, a big city. It will take five years to turn it around.

> ALAN BALL, City manager, 1995.

I went over to the Bury fans and said 'Look on the bright side. You could be supporting Manchester City.'

> RICHIE BOND, Blyth Spartans player, after scoring
> in the non-Leaguers' FA Cup win, 1995.

Check out the details about the second largest Manchester club.

> BLURB on dustcover of *Manchester City FC – An A to Z*,
> by Dean Hayes, 1995.

MANCHESTER UNITED

A Manchester United player has to want the ball, have the courage to want the ball. He's a player with imagination, someone who has the big picture.

> ALEX FERGUSON, United manager, 1995.

I value truth, honesty, respect for one another, compassion and understanding. I have found these qualities in Manchester United.

ERIC CANTONA, from La Philosophie de Cantona, 1995.

This has been a love story. It is something that is strong for me. The love of the club is the most important weapon in the world. I just couldn't leave.

CANTONA explaining his decision to stay at Old Trafford, 1995.

It's like being in a palace, an overwhelming and inspiring place. For me it came as a culture shock – even the loos have gold taps.

GARRY BIRTLES, former United striker, 1993.

Since I came to England I have seen broken jaws, broken legs and horrendous tackles, but most times they involved nonentities and they didn't fill newspapers. With my team no opponent has been carried off on a stretcher with injuries like this. No gashes, no nothing.

FERGUSON, defending his players against criticism, 1995.

I was sitting there, level with their front line and I looked across at Giggs, Sharpe, Cantona and Kanchelskis. Awesome. Anyone who plays like that deserves to win things.

KEVIN KEEGAN, Newcastle manager, after draw at St James' Park, 1993.

We have been winning right through the Nineties. Now there is the pain of defeat, and it's showing. It was good to see that. Sometimes the players forget what losing is like. They only remember being winners. The alternative experience can help the team develop.

FERGUSON, after United missed out on Premiership
and FA Cup in eight days, 1995.

I hate losing. It stinks.

PETER SCHMEICHEL, United goalkeeper after
Wembley defeat, 1995.

It took me an hour to get the scorch marks off the turf.

KEITH KENT, United groundsman, after brilliant display v Bolton, 1995.

United have some great players, but in the likes of Eric Cantona, Mark Hughes, Bryan Robson, Roy Keane, Steve Bruce and Peter Schmeichel, they have men who can play a rough-house game.

DAVE BASSETT, Sheffield United manager, 1993.

Less than a month after thousands of youngsters pulled on their favourite club jersey at Christmas, the men who run the club ordered the Red Devils to trot out in blue at Southampton. Loyalty doesn't seem to be enough any more. Rather it is exploited to make us pay more.

TONY BLAIR MP, Labour leader, criticising United's commercialism, 1995.

If he's looking for a beacon to see how clubs should be run, he should be looking at Manchester United and not making cheap shots.

KEN RAMSDEN, United assistant secretary, replying to Blair, 1995.

One of the country's finest grounds. Huge video screens bring constant updates showing United's progress on the FTSE, Dow Jones and Nikkei markets throughout the match.

THE ONION BAG magazine, 1993.

We're a massive club but I've never seen anything like the United Megastore. The queues to get in the shop would fill Walsall's ground.

ANDY TOWNSEND, Aston Villa midfielder, 1995.

Manchester United plc? It means Premier League Champions, of course.

TERRY CHRISTIAN, compere, Channel 4's The Word, 1995.

MIDDLESBROUGH

Our long-term aim is to make Middlesbrough synonymous with a good team rather than cooling towers and chemical works. I think we're well on our way, even though Ruud Gullit had never heard of us when we contacted him in the summer.

STEVE GIBSON, chairman, 1995.

MILLWALL

Earthquakes, wars and Millwall – results as they happen.

RADIO 5 LIVE advertising campaign, 1994.

Then I came to Millwall, a club with a chip on both shoulders.

MICK McCARTHY, Republic of Ireland and former Millwall manager, 1996.

I met a pal who lost track of me after Celtic and asked me what I was doing. I said I was player-manager at Millwall. His wife immediately said: 'How embarrassing!'

McCARTHY, 1995.

We have played for some of the great clubs in Europe, but we regard this as the pinnacle of our careers.

SERGEI YURAN, Spartak Moscow striker, on joining the south London club with Vassili Kulkov, 1996.

NEWCASTLE UNITED

Tell Alex (Ferguson) we're coming to get him.

KEVIN KEEGAN, manager, celebrating promotion, 1993.

I wanted to take a sick club and make it better. It's always easier to raise something from the ashes. I wanted to be a football doctor. And that's what I was at first – I was asked to cure a very sick patient.

KEEGAN, 1995.

Newcastle is light years away from what the club was when Gazza was here – the club is probably too big for him now.

SIR JOHN HALL, chairman, 1995.

We are like the Basques. We are fighting for a nation, the Geordie nation. Football means so much to us, it's part of our lives. Football is tribalism and we're the Mohicans.

SIR JOHN HALL, Newcastle chairman, 1995.

It's too far north.

JOHN SALAKO, Crystal Palace winger, turning down move to Newcastle, 1995.

NIGERIA

We were complaining to the referee at the time Maradona took the free-kick. But we're learning fast – next time, we'll hold the ball while we talk.

RASHIDI YEKINI, Nigeria striker, after World Cup game v Argentina, 1994.

NORTHAMPTON TOWN

I was very influenced by watching Northampton when they won the Fourth Division.

JACK CHARLTON, Ireland manager, on the roots of the Republic's style, 1994.
Northampton went from Fourth to First in the
Sixties (and back again).

RAITH ROVERS

Highlight of my time there was half-time in the Olympic Stadium in Munich. The thought of Klinsmann and the rest in the Bayern dressing-room getting a bollocking because we were beating them 1-0 – I have a wee smile when I think about that.

JIMMY NICHOLL, Millwall manager, 1996. Raith lost 2-1 to Bayern.

RANGERS

All over the world it would have been a penalty. But at Ibrox it wasn't.

IVAN GOLAC, Dundee United manager, after being denied a 'blatant' penalty
against Rangers, 1994. United, leading at the time, lost 2-1.

It's good to be with a really big European club again.

BASILE BOLI, French international defender, on leaving Rangers
for Monaco, 1995.

REPUBLIC OF IRELAND

A lot of Jack's (Charlton) players are happy to be picked for the Republic because they couldn't find a way of making it with England or Scotland.

BILLY BINGHAM, Northern Ireland manager, 1993.

What Billy has said is a scandal. When I was first picked for Ireland it was not the pounds sign which flashed before my eyes, but the shamrock.

JOHN ALDRIDGE, Merseyside-born striker with the Republic, 1993.

As the first bars ring out I notice the TV camera starting to zoom in. Should I move my lips and sing the two or three lines that I know?

ANDY TOWNSEND, Republic of Ireland captain, on an Anglo-Irishman's difficulty with the national anthem, in *Andy's Game*, 1994.

Italy turn up in Armani suits looking the dog's bollocks and we turn up in bright green blazers and dodgy brogues.

PHIL BABB, Liverpool and Republic of Ireland defender, 1995.

The Republic have just one game plan. If Plan A fails, resort to Plan A.

MARK LAWRENSON, former Ireland defender on their costly failures against Liechtenstein and Austria, 1995.

They play football on the second floor.

LITHUANIAN player after match v Republic, 1994.

Opponents used to come up to me during games and say: 'Ireland do not play football. It is rugby'. I'd reply: 'Yeah, but we're winning 2-1'.

MICK McCARTHY, Millwall manager and Jack Charlton's successor, 1995.

SCARBOROUGH

If only our motto, 'No Battle No Victory' wasn't taken a little too literally at times.

MARK STANIFORTH, Scarborough supporter, 1995.

SCOTLAND

Bagpipes and claymores won't win us games in the European Championship or World Cup.

CRAIG BROWN, Scotland manager, 1994.

People expect us to beat everybody we play. The trouble is, so do I.

BROWN, Scotland manager, after defeat by United States, 1996.

SHEFFIELD UNITED

When you look at the tip opposite our main stand, it's almost as if some of Fred West's bodies are under there and we can't build until they're dug up.

DAVE BASSETT, Sheffield United manager,
on Bramall Lane's perenially unbuilt stand, 1995.

When I was a lad, when we played Wednesday, they'd wear blue and white stripes and we'd wear red and white stripes. Now they wear all sorts of stuff, like a fashion parade. Where have our stripes gone this season? Blades' strip look as if it was designed by Julian Clary when he had a migraine.

SEAN BEAN, actor and Sheffield United fan, 1996.

STOKE CITY

We ground out a result. We're a grinding team from a working-class area.

LOU MACARI, Stoke manager, after 1-0 win over Millwall, 1995.

STONEWALL

The Queens of South London.

DAILY MIRROR headline 'outing' the gays-only club, 1995.

I remember telling one of my previous team I was starving and could kill a plate of sausage and chips. One player just looked at me and said: 'I should think you get enough sausage already, don't you?'

PAUL BARKER, Stonewall captain, 1995.

TOTTENHAM HOTSPUR

When (Ilie) Dumitrescu asked me when Spurs last won the championship I couldn't answer him. That shouldn't be the case for a club this big.

OSSIE ARDILES, Tottenham manager, 1994.

They might have first option on me, but I'd sooner sign for Grimsby than Tottenham.

PAUL GASCOIGNE on British interest during his final days at Lazio, 1995.

I don't think Spurs would ever sign a superstar like Klinsmann or a Bergkamp again. Those guys are floaters. They'll go anywhere, play for anyone who pays them the most.

ALAN SUGAR, Tottenham chairman, after Arsenal paid £7.25m for Bergkamp, 1995.

WIMBLEDON

The best way to watch Wimbledon is on Ceefax.

GARY LINEKER, TV pundit, 1993.

Their chairman did no credit at all to the club. He wrote absolute filth all over the dressing-room wall.

BILLY BONDS, West Ham manager, after Sam Hammam left Wimbledon's calling card at Upton Park, 1993.

They are kicking the ball 50 yards instead of 60.

MIKE WALKER, Norwich manager, on Wimbledon's reported change of style, 1993.

I told him that his season ticket was not a prison sentence and gave him his money back.

SAM HAMMAM, Wimbledon owner, on a critical supporter, 1995.

The rich are getting richer, and we're getting detached. In the end it's not the ability of any other club or lack of desire that will kill us – the cheque book will.

JOE KINNEAR, manager, advocating a move to Dublin, 1995.

WOLVERHAMPTON WANDERERS

Bring back the Fifties!

WOLVES FANS' CHANT at Molineux during demonstration against Graham Taylor, 1995.

There are only four clubs I'd have considered leaving Leicester for — Manchester United, Newcastle, Rangers and Wolves. This is the last of the sleeping giants.

MARK McGHEE, Wolves manager, 1995.

Before the new stadium was built the place was a health hazard. The dressing room leaked, we were always mopping up and there were cockroaches doing backstroke in the bath.

KEITH DOWNING, Wolves midfielder, on leaving for Birmingham, 1993.

CHAPTER 2

Just About Managing

A lot of managers rejoice in stupidity...For the few very bright ones there's an awful lot who don't bring any credit to the sport. Can you think of any other trade in the latter part of the 20th century where they call their superiors 'gaffer' or 'boss'. I think that's pathetic.

JON HOLMES, players' agent, 1996.

One thing I've learned since becoming a manager is that in the public's minds, players win games and managers lose them.

BRYAN ROBSON, Middlesbrough player-manager, 1995.

The manager gets too much credit when things go well, and too much blame when they don't.

GRAHAM TAYLOR, England manager, 1994.

There's only two types of manager. Those who've been sacked and those who will be sacked in the future.

HOWARD WILKINSON, Leeds manager, 1995.

Managers have got a sixth sense about these things, like wounded elephants going to their graves to die.

TONY HALE, West Bromwich Albion chairman, after the departure of Keith Burkinshaw, 1994.

I told the chairman that if he ever wants to sack me, all he has to do is take me into town, buy me a meal, a few pints and a cigar, and I'll piss off.

MICK McCARTHY, Millwall manager, 1995.

We've all been through it. You've never really been a manager until you've been sacked.

BRIAN HORTON, Manchester City manager, on taking over from Peter Reid, 1993.

You just have to wait for someone to suffer the same misfortune as you. It's a unique situation in that you can actually study the job vacancies on Teletext as they happen.

GRAHAM TURNER, Hereford United director of football, 1995.

If a manager goes through a red light these days he's liable to get the sack. Of course I have worries on that score. Al Capone had more friends than I've got at the moment.

HOWARD WILKINSON, under pressure at Leeds, 1994.

The richest managers are the ones who've failed and got a pay-off.

BOBBY GOULD, Coventry manager, on why he worked
without a contract, 1993.

Managing is a very stressful job. It doesn't matter how many you've won, on Saturday evening you get half an hour of satisfaction before the pressure starts again.

CHRIS NICHOLL, Walsall manager, 1996.

I simply wasn't prepared to commit myself for seven days a week. In any walk of life, people want more leisure time.

KENNY DALGLISH, on moving 'upstairs' from the job of manager at Blackburn
to becoming Director of Football, 1995.

I was on a drip in a hospital bed and this player came to see me. I thought he was enquiring about my health. He never even asked how I was. All he was interested in was how he stood regarding his contract. He'd even brought his agent in.

JOHN McCLELLAND, former St Johnstone manager, on one of the factors
behind his decision to quit, 1995.

How many games have I got left? Is it one or two after that performance?

BRIAN HORTON, Manchester City manager,
after 0-0 draw with Coventry, 1995.

As a manager, it's your head on the block. You've got to make cold-blooded decisions and if you can't then you shouldn't be in the job. To be honest, I found it difficult to be a bastard.

TERRY BUTCHER, former Coventry and Sunderland manager, 1994.

As a manager, you always have a gun to your head. It's a question of whether there is a bullet in the barrel.

KEVIN KEEGAN, Newcastle manager, anticipating trouble after selling Andy Cole, 1995.

You only need one to fire the bullet, you don't need a firing squad.

ALAN SMITH, Crystal Palace manager, as his relationship with chairman
Ron Noades approached its inevitable conclusion,1995.

Seven games we've lost 1-0, another seven we've drawn 0-0. If we'd drawn the 1-0 games we lost, we'd have another seven points. If the seven goalless draws had been 1-0 to us we would have 28 points more and be third in the Premiership.

SMITH, during Palace's slide towards relegation, 1995.

Maybe I'll have to change my way of thinking. I work for the long, long term but sometimes you have to survive the short term first.

OSSIE ARDILES, former Tottenham manager, after his sacking
by Mexican club Guadalajara, 1995.

When we lost at Carlisle I was mulling it all over on the bus, reliving every kick, and I could hear the players playing cards and laughing. It's not that they don't care, but they soon forget, whereas for a manager it's a seven-day punishment.

ANDY KING, Mansfield manager, 1994.

Thank God I have a good family and I'm financially secure. Sometimes I say to myself: 'Is it really worth it? Do I want to go on?' You have to be a kind of Robocop to do this job.

CARLOS ALBERTO PARREIRA, Brazil coach, before World Cup finals, 1994.

A lot of people are happy being No. 2, the assistant or the coach. They look at the manager's job and think 'I can do that'. Then suddenly they get there, with absolute control, and the buck stopping with them. Then they understand the pressure.

HARRY REDKNAPP, West Ham manager, 1995.

My electrician's exam was much tougher than this.

JIMMY CASE, Brighton manager, on the pressures
of his new job, 1995.

I did take a week's holiday, but standing in the sunshine watching the lads train pre-season, that's my holiday.

BARRY FRY, Birmingham manager, 1995.

I have thought about being a manager. When you're young you think it would be an impossible job, then when you get older you realise it's not what it's cracked up to be.

JOHN BARNES, Liverpool and England midfielder, 1995.

I always thought managers were more involved, but when it comes down to it, I just sit there and watch like everyone else.

KEVIN KEEGAN, Newcastle manager, 1993.

There are grounds when you know you'll be covered in spittle and you wear your old clothes.

DAVE BASSETT, Sheffield United manager, to Graham Taylor, Wolves manager,
after he was attacked at Bramall Lane, 1995.

It has got to the stage where I thought I was being followed in my car. There was even a threat to kidnap me and take me to a zoo, but it didn't materialise.

IAN BRANFOOT, Southampton manager, on the public campaign
to oust him, 1993.

What I hope, and this is being a bit selfish, is that if and when it does come to an end here (Aston Villa), it isn't like it was at Leicester. I worked my socks off there for three years and now I'll probably never get an ounce of credit.

BRIAN LITTLE, Villa manager, on his parting with Leicester, 1995.

Look at you lot. You're all sick as pigs, aren't you? You're only here because you expected them to knock us over.

KENNY HIBBITT, Cardiff manager, to the press after his
team's FA Cup win at non-League Rushden & Diamonds, 1995.

I've reached a stage in life where I don't give a bugger what the press write about me as long as it's not slanderous.

RON ATKINSON, Coventry manager, 1995.

The ref gave a goal against us (by Arsenal) and as I turned around I saw this big furry microphone so I laid into it. I kicked it and it went spinning around like a boomerang and landed 20 yards away. Then the Sky touchline reporter came up to me and said: 'So Mick, you must be disappointed'.

MICK McCARTHY, Millwall manager, 1995.

It's a lot of work, this job. I got a phone call at five o'clock this morning from a journalist in India.

JACK CHARLTON, Republic of Ireland manager,
at the World Cup finals, 1994.

I've spent more money on my car since I became manager than I have on players.

JIM FALLON, Dumbarton manager, 1995.

I'd like to go through all the usual cliches, only it was worse than that.

ROY EVANS, Liverpool manager, after last-minute defeat at Newcastle, 1995.

It may sound daft, but until we let in those three goals before half-time I thought we were the better side.

ROLY HOWARD, manager of non-League Marine,
beaten 11-2 at Shrewsbury in the FA Cup, 1995.

They let the club down.

STEVE PATERSON, Caledonian Thistle manager,
after his team's 6-1 defeat of Albion Rovers, 1995.
Paterson thought his players had soft-pedalled.

I don't follow the transfer market in case it depresses me.

DARIO GRADI, Crewe Alexandra manager, 1995.

Because of our financial situation I spent my first three months here trying to do swap deals. Funny how other managers always want to exchange one of their reserves for your best player.

MURDO MacLEOD, Partick Thistle manager, 1996.

Q: If you won the Lottery what would you buy?
A: 27 new strikers.

BARRY FRY, Birmingham manager, in programme questionnaire, 1996.

Q: Are funds available for new players?
A: Oh yes. About £2.54.

IAN BRANFOOT, Fulham manager, at post-match press conference, 1994.

To be manager of a Third Division club and find yourself on a plane to Barcelona on a scouting mission is the stuff dreams are made of.

GRAHAM BARROW, Wigan Athletic manager, on signing Seba, Martinez and Diaz, Wigan's 'three amigos', 1995.

I'm the man for the job. I can revive our World Cup hopes. Anyway, I couldn't do a worse job, could I?

SCREAMING LORD SUTCH, leader of the Monster Raving Loony Party, on why he should succeed Graham Taylor as England manager, 1993.

I've worked for the last three England managers and I've seen what it did to them. I saw Ron Greenwood break out in sores, Bobby Robson go grey, and poor Graham Taylor double up in anguish and stick his head between his legs so far it nearly disappeared up his backside. If I was single, with no kids, it'd be no problem, but I've a wife and three children and I've seen the effect the job can have on your family. It won't happen to mine.

HOWARD WILKINSON, Leeds manager, after Taylor's exit, 1993.

The England manager has got to fight the system and he's got to fight the press from day one.

WILKINSON, 1993.

I wouldn't take the England job for a big gold clock.

STEVE COPPELL, former Crystal Palace manager, 1993.

Even the Pope would think twice about taking that job.

ROY HODGSON, Switzerland manager, 1993.

As manager of the national team, you know that, apart from the Chancellor, you will probably be the most hated man in the country.

OSSIE ARDILES, Tottenham manager, disclaiming interest in the England job, 1993.

The only way I'd be interested in the England job is as a player-manager.

RON ATKINSON, Aston Villa manager, 1993.

Managing England should be the best job in the world but it has become a horrible job...To think of my children going into school and getting hammered in the playground because their dad is England manager. Perhaps we should be looking for a guy who is divorced with no kids.

GLENN HODDLE, then Chelsea player-manager, 1994.

I'm authorised to say on behalf of the FA that Terry Venables does not need votes of confidence from us. We all know how they are interpreted in football.

DAVID DAVIES, FA director of public affairs, as criticism of Venables' court cases surfaced inside the FA, 1995.

I lost consciousness 20 minutes from the end.

TOMMY BURNS, Kilmarnock player-manager, after turning out against Rangers in his 38th year, 1994.

I've just been given a video recording of the game, and I'm going to tape *Neighbours* over it.

HARRY REDKNAPP, West Ham manager, after 0-0 draw with Southampton, 1995.

I've been at Port Vale 16 years. Even the Great Train Robbers didn't get that long a sentence. Here you are manager, coach, chief scout, chief cook and bottle washer, but I've loved every minute of it.

JOHN RUDGE, Port Vale manager, 1996.

I'm healthy, I've got a house, I eat well – how can I be unhappy. There's thousands out there with none of those things.

HOWARD WILKINSON, Leeds manager, 1993.

I'm not a politician, a social worker or a clergyman. I'm a provider of distraction and fans want to go back home happy to whatever bores the arse off them in the week.

WILKINSON, 1994.

You have to be a bit of everything these days: coach, social worker, the lot. If Claire Rayner knew soccer, she'd be a great manager.

MICK McCARTHY, Millwall manager, 1995.

Only being the manager stopped me punching him.

BRIAN LAWS, Grimsby player-manager, after Leicester's Garry Parker – a former Nottingham
Forest team-mate – ruffled his hair at the end of fraught match, 1995.

That ranting and raving stuff goes in one ear and out the other. If you talk to people, they'll listen.

RAY WILKINS, QPR player-manager, on his man-management style, 1995.

A coach is like a winemaker. He must produce the best wine from the grapes he has available.

FABIO CAPELLO, Milan coach, on life after Gullit,
Rijkaard and Van Basten, 1993.

There's no difference between coaching England and coaching Newbury Town. The reason is that they're all blokes. There are England blokes, Manchester United blokes, Arsenal blokes and Newbury blokes. You are coaching men, human beings.

DON HOWE, who worked with both the national team
and his local Isthmian League part-timers, 1994.

Coaching is for kids. If a player can't trap a ball and pass it by the time he's in the team, he shouldn't be there in the first place. (At Derby) I told Roy McFarland to go out and get his bloody hair cut – that's coaching at top level.

BRIAN CLOUGH, former Nottingham Forest manager, 1994.

It's going to be strange not going into training at Chadwell Heath every day. I think my car will go there by itself in the morning.

BILLY BONDS on resigning as West Ham manager
after 27 years at the club, 1994.

I'm still the best five-a-side player at the club. Mind you, as someone said, that's probably why we're in the position we're in.

RON ATKINSON, 56-year-old manager of Coventry,
then bottom of the Premiership, 1995.

I had to look around to make sure there were no players about. I was worried about having me pants whipped off by some of the lads, so I made sure I was near the tunnel when I did it, and then legged it quick. I got a lot of stick from me wife for not having new pants on.

DAVE BASSETT, Sheffield United manager, after giving his tracksuit trousers
to a fan at last home game, 1994-95.

Players don't want to retire and be managers any more. They want to be Directors of Football – that's definitely the one to have. Pick your games, keep an eye on the rest, no real pressure. Come in on a Saturday, sit in the boardroom, nice cup of tea, nice gin and tonic. Say: 'Well, this is the way I'd do it. Anyway, I'm off.' In the meantime, the manager is sitting on the bench shouting and screaming like an idiot. I know what I'd rather have.

HARRY REDKNAPP, West Ham manager, 1995.

I can't see West Ham going for a Director of Football though. Director of Traffic, maybe.

REDKNAPP, 1995.

You heard that booing at the end? Well I started it.

RON ATKINSON, Aston Villa manager, after home defeat by Oldham, 1994.

Welcome to the Grey Hair Club.

MESSAGE from Kevin Keegan to John Aldridge when he became
Tranmere player-manager, 1996.

CHAPTER 3

The Gaffer

OSSIE ARDILES

REPORTER: Is Klinsmann Spurs' biggest-ever signing?
OSSIE ARDILES: No, I was.

EXCHANGE at press conference to unveil
Tottenham's German capture, 1995.

RON ATKINSON

The only relaxed boss is Big Ron. He had me drinking pink champagne – before a match.

HARRY REDKNAPP, West Ham manager, 1995.

There is this champagne-and-nightclubs image that he has, but above all he loves the game and the company of football people. He's still a child at heart. In training this season he's been everyone from Arnold Muhren to David Ginola.

GORDON STRACHAN, Coventry player-coach, 1996.

Just think, Barbra Streisand and Ron Atkinson at Wembley in the same year. Win, lose or draw it's got to be a great season.

ATKINSON, then Aston Villa manager,
before Coca-Cola Cup final, 1994.

Q: What was the highlight of your World Cup?
A: Bumping into Frank Sinatra at the Friday night concert in L.A. I turned the corner with Gary Newbon, and there he was with Bob Hope.

ATKINSON, at the World Cup finals as ITV summariser, 1994.

My missus reckons that if people don't recognise me in the street, I go back and tell them who I am.

ATKINSON, after becoming Coventry manager, 1995.

They call him Big Ron because he is a big spender in the transfer market. I just call him Fat Ron.

MALCOLM ALLISON, Bristol Rovers acting manager, before FA Cup tie, 1993.

ALAN BALL

He is a Judas. He spent last season preaching loyalty and integrity then leaves the first time a cheque is waved in front of him.

NICK ILLINGWORTH, Southampton fans' spokesman, 1995.

There were situations when Alan Ball and I didn't see eye to eye, and it had nothing to do with me being 6ft 4in and him being 5ft 3in.

DAVE BEASANT, Southampton goalkeeper, 1995.

I fancy Bally to survive this season for two main reasons. The first is he is a mate of the chairman. The second is that if Franny Lee sacks two bosses in six months, he will be up there with Peter Swales in the making-a-pig's-ear-of it stakes.

JIMMY GREAVES, former England team-mate, in his *Sun* column, 1995.

Alan Ball's a football genius.

MANCHESTER CITY FANS' CHANT as their team climbed off foot of the Premiership, 1995.

DAVE BASSETT

A lot of my friends grew up with me through football, so now they all call me Harry. Even my wife does – it's only when she calls me Dave that I know I'm in the shit.

BASSETT, Sheffield United manager, on the origins of his nickname, 1995.

CRAIG BROWN

I was wearing my tracksuit bottoms when Craig Brown (Scotland coach under Andy Roxburgh) told me to take them off. 'All the players have to look the same,' he told me. I pointed out how cold it was and kept them on. I don't think he ever forgave me.

> RICHARD GOUGH, Rangers and former Scotland captain, recalling a national team training session in Belgium in 1987, in *Field of Dreams*, 1994.

Charisma comes from results and not vice versa.

> BROWN, Scotland manager, on criticism that the team needed a 'personality' manager, 1993.

Bob has three degrees from universities, including one in North Carolina, Jock is an MA from Cambridge and I'm a BA from the Open University. As a footballer I was the one the manager would turn to last and say: 'Right son, nothing clever from you this week'.

> BROWN, 1995.
> Bob and Jock are the Scotland manager's brothers.

Q: Most dangerous moment?
A: Half-time with Craig Brown.

> GERRY CREANEY, Celtic striker, recalling clash with the then Scotland Under-21 coach, in newspaper questionnaire, 1993.

JACK CHARLTON

Greg Rusedski? Who's he? If you're going to find a Brit you might as well go for the best. Jack Charlton would have got us Pete Sampras.

> DESMOND LYNAM, presenter, during BBC-TV coverage of Wimbledon tennis, 1994.

We like Jack. He's a crazy man but we need characters in football. However, he must learn where to draw a line with his behaviour.

> GUIDO TOGNONI, Fifa spokesman, after Charlton's touchline ban, World Cup finals, 1994.

We kept expecting bags or bottles or water to come flying down from the top of the grandstand and explode around our ankles.

> ANDY TOWNSEND, Republic of Ireland captain, during the ban.

IF I WAS A PUNTER I'D RATHER HAVE KENNY DALGLISH TOO.

CRAIG BROWN, Scotland manager, 1994.

Thanks Jack, you have been a manager in a million.

> LOUIS KILCOYNE, president, FA of Ireland,
> accepting Charlton's resignation, 1995.

You go in a pub and they used to have pictures of John F Kennedy or the Pope on the walls. Now it's Jack everywhere.

> NIALL QUINN, Republic of Ireland striker, on Charlton's retirement, 1995.

Imagine what Ireland might have done if led and inspired by a man of vision and courage. This is not very hard to do: remember Giants Stadium, when with the spur of an early goal, the players overcame miserable tactics to humble Italy.

> EAMON DUNPHY, former Republic player, in the *Independent on Sunday*
> after what proved Charlton's final match, 1995.

BRIAN CLOUGH

At first I thought it was a bundle of rubbish, but then I realised it was Brian Clough.

> DAVID GADD, Derbyshire fireman, finding Clough having a rest
> in a field near his home, 1993.

Old Big 'Ead has had enough.

> CLOUGH announcing his retirement as Nottingham Forest manager, 1993.

He's gone, thank heaven!

> DR GEORGE WATERHOUSE, Forest director,
> at club's AGM, 1993.

He always insisted on addressing me as Edward. I told him I'd always been known as Teddy but it didn't make a blind bit of difference.

> TEDDY SHERINGHAM, Tottenham striker, recalling his Forest days, 1995.

He gave by far the best interview of all the candidates – confident, passionate, full of common sense and, above all, patriotic. If Ron Greenwood hadn't been around, he'd have clinched it.

> PETER SWALES, former FA international committee chairman,
> on Clough's application to manage England 17 years earlier, 1995.

They didn't want an England manager who was prepared to call the Italians cheating bastards. They failed to understand that I would have curbed my language and revelled in the relief from the day-to-day, month-by-month grind of club management.

CLOUGH, 1994.

I'm ill-tempered, rude and wondering what's for tea. Just the same as always.

CLOUGH on what he is like around 4.45pm on Saturdays, 1994.

The pigeons in Derby will welcome the news. There'll be more room on my head to shit on than anyone else.

CLOUGH on the decision of the City of Derby to erect a statue in his honour, 1995.

KENNY DALGLISH

I've always felt there's a scriptwriter up on a cloud somewhere who has been penning Kenny's life story. He just seems to pop up in the most in incredible places to create history.

GORDON STRACHAN, Coventry assistant manager, on his former Scotland team-mate's championship success with Blackburn, 1995.

He's a good manager, there's no doubt that he's done well, but is he any better than somebody at the bottom of the League or is it because he's got £30m to spend on players? That is the difference. It's about having money.

HARRY REDKNAPP, West Ham manager, 1995.

He's been a very lucky young man. You see, unlike some of us managers, he hasn't had to sweat and toil for his living.

BRIAN CLOUGH, former Nottingham Forest manager, in his *News of the World* column, 1995.

To a degree he has marketed the dour image to protect himself.

GRAEME LE SAUX, Blackburn player under Dalglish's management, 1995.

Kenny's such a football nut that you could mention the name of *any* player playing in England and he'd know who you were talking about.

ALAN HANSEN, former Liverpool colleague and TV pundit, 1993.

We won 2-1 and I was made up afterwards. Then the door opens and Kenny Dalglish is standing there. 'Are you the groundsman? I've got some advice for you – save up and buy a bloody mower!' I said: 'Mr Dalglish, when I'm working for Liverpool I'll prepare pitches for Liverpool to play on, but while I'm working here I'll prepare them for Crewe'. Christ! He slammed the door so hard it nearly came off its hinges. I don't suppose I'll get a job at Ewood Park now.

JOHN HUXLEY, Crewe Alexandra groundsman,
recalling a pre-season friendly, 1995.

He has an aura but is also very down to earth. He is not a complete disciplinarian, as a lot of people think. He uses psychology: when you're injured he won't even speak to you, won't ask how you are. I think it comes from Bill Shankly: 'You're no use to me if you're injured'. Not even with Alan Shearer, at least not in front of the other players. That's football – it's the law of the jungle. It can be lonely.

GRAEME LE SAUX, 1994.

What has Dalglish done? He decides he doesn't want to stand in the tunnel any more with his brown overcoat on. He wants to sit up there with the directors. That's certainly not a crime but I'll tell you what: it's an abdication of his managerial responsibilities.

BRIAN CLOUGH, on Dalglish's move 'upstairs' at Blackburn,
in his *News of the World* column, 1995.

ALEX FERGUSON

I can meet ministers and monarchs and my children are not much impressed, but when we met Alex Ferguson they realised there was some point.

TONY BLAIR MP, Leader of the Labour Party, 1995.

I hope my reputation doesn't have to be judged on Eric Cantona's life with Manchester United. If that's the only blip in my career, I'll accept it and go happily to the big penalty box in the sky.

FERGUSON, Manchester United manager, 1995.

I don't think there's any person in the game who could do the job.

FERGUSON on the difficulties of the Old Trafford hot seat, 1995.

He did (at Aberdeen) what he's still doing at United. He gave us a persecution complex about Celtic and Rangers, the Scottish FA and the Glasgow media; the whole West of Scotland thing. He reckoned they were all against us, and it worked a treat.

> MARK McGHEE, Leicester manager and former Aberdeen striker, 1995.

You see Fergie on the touchline nowadays and he's laughing and smiling. It's like watching a fan having a great time.

> PAT CRERAND, former United midfielder, on the change in Ferguson after the championship breakthrough, 1994.

My heart is with United, but I can't stay for one reason – and that's the manager.

> ANDREI KANCHELSKIS, United's Russian international winger, shortly before joining Everton, 1995.

I'm not getting involved in that. I'm a man of repute now. In fact, I don't know why I'm talking to you lot.

> FERGUSON to journalists after receiving the OBE, 1995.

Alex always had a hot temper. He'd have caused a fight in an empty house.

> MARTIN FERGUSON, younger brother, 1995.

ALEX FERGUSON: Five hours' sleep is all I need.
INTERVIEWER: Like Margaret Thatcher.
FERGUSON: Don't associate me with that woman.

> EXCHANGE at press interview, 1995.

BARRY FRY

He should be called Small Fry.

> JOE KINNEAR, Wimbledon manager, after dispute over transfer deal, 1995.

I love Barry Fry as all managers do but he has a disease he can't do anything about – he talks about private things when he shouldn't.

> DAVID PLEAT, Sheffield Wednesday manager, on the Birmingham manager's tendency to conduct transfers in public, 1996.

I couldn't give a monkey's what the opposition do, all I worry about is what we do when we've got the ball. Sometimes it works, sometimes it doesn't. I've done it that way since I was at Dunstable. I wouldn't do it any different if I was managing England.

FRY, 1995.

His management style seems to be based on the chaos theory.

MARK McGHEE, Wolves manager, 1996.

He acts as though he is in charge of *The Magic Roundabout*.

GEOFF DUNFORD, Bristol Rovers vice-chairman, 1996.

I wish Barry Fry was England manager. Just think of it, we could all get a game.

LETTER to *Evening Mail*, Birmingham, after Fry took his tally of signings to 55 in 27 months, 1996.

Kirstine's out shopping as usual. I'm down the JobCentre looking for employment. Funny old game, innit?

FRY ansaphone message after being sacked by Birmingham, 1996.

If you want to speak to Barry you'll get him at United at 10 o'clock. If you're wondering what's happened to Fergie, nothing has. It's not Man United, it's Peterborough United. Sensational news. Funny old game, innit?

FRY ansaphone message on re-emerging as co-owner and manager of Peterborough, 1996.

BOBBY GOULD

He's a bit like Picasso, the painter — he does things other people don't even think of.

SAM HAMMAM, Wimbledon owner, after Gould's sudden departure from Coventry, 1993.

He would make a smashing double-glazing salesman. We had a meeting last night and by the end of it, we thought: 'When's he going to sell us a new car?'

NEVILLE SOUTHALL, Wales goalkeeper, on his country's new manager, 1995.

GEORGE GRAHAM

He comes into the dressing-room like Moses carrying the tabloids.

ANONYMOUS Arsenal player, 1994.

Mogadon Man of the Year

TELETEXT nomination, 1994.

There's no way George Graham will be a scapegoat. There may be a fair bit of pain to go through yet and I don't know why I feel like the man who shot Bambi.

RICK PARRY, chief executive of the FA Premier League, pledging to cast the anti-corruption net beyond the former Arsenal manager, 1995.

Mr Graham did not act in the best interests of the club.

ARSENAL statement announcing Graham's dismissal following the 'bung' investigation, 1995.

I deeply regret that this kangaroo-court judgement should have been reached in such a hole-in-the-corner way. My record of loyalty and service demanded better treatment.

GRAHAM, on being sacked, 1995.

The meeting (with Rune Hauge) was all very normal but the money came as a shock. I thought: 'Jesus, what a Christmas present – fantastic'.

GRAHAM on receiving the 'gift' of £140,500 from Norwegian agent Hauge, 1995.

Deep down I had a gut feeling the gifts could bring complications, but I didn't know the tremors would register on the Richter scale. The ridiculous thing is it wouldn't have changed my life. I was on a good salary, but greed got the better of me. Now I wish I'd never clapped eyes on Rune Hauge.

GRAHAM, 1995.

As a respected manager of a Premier League team and a senior figure in the League Managers' Association, he must have known just how serious a matter it was for him to be receiving this amount of money from an agent.

FA STATEMENT rejecting Graham's plea that he had done nothing wrong in accepting £425,000 from Hauge, 1995.

The suggestion that George be stripped of the honour (freeman of Islington) came from the lone Conservative councillor, which was a typically mean and petty-minded view.

ALAN CLINTON, Leader of Islington Council, 1995.

A revealing and honest examination of the workings of a big club.

MIDDLESBROUGH EVENING GAZETTE's review of Graham's book
The Grief and The Glory, 1995.

World According to Boy from Barlinnie

HEADLINE in The Independent on review of Graham's autobiography, 1996.
Graham is from Bargeddie, some distance from Glasgow's
infamous Barlinnie Prison.

I have never claimed to be a knight in shining armour. I am as weak as the next man when it comes to temptation.

GRAHAM admitting he was 'stupid' and 'greedy' to accept Hauge's 'bung', 1995.

I think as soon as this is all over, round about next January or February, they will be out head-hunting me.

GRAHAM looking forward hopefully to a future in football, 1995.

I'm going to do another book in five years' time. It's going to be called The Glory, The Grief and The Glory.

GRAHAM, promising a comeback after publication of
The Grief and The Glory during his year's ban, 1995.

GLENN HODDLE

He's our first really good manager, a manager other people would like to have, since Dave Sexton left in 1973.

MATTHEW HARDING, Chelsea director and benefactor, 1995.

He's got a very, very tough persona, despite the fact that they used to call him Glenda.

PETER SHREEVES, Hoddle's No 2 at Chelsea
and his ex-manager at Spurs, 1996.

The boss of Chelsea has just become England boss. There's a good sign.

> JOHN MAJOR, Prime Minister, looking for good omens after
> bad local election results for the Tories, 1996.

ROY HODGSON

Terry (Venables) has a choice of Gascoigne, Platt, Beardsley and Ince. Any of those would be in the Swiss side. I've got to pick between Sforza, Sforza and Sforza. I usually pick Sforza.

> HODGSON, Switzerland coach, on the limitations of his squad
> compared with England's, 1995.

The lasting memory I have of him is that he always had a very runny nose.

> DAVE MOGG, Bath City goalkeeper, after Hodgson, once his manager at Bristol City,
> took over at Inter Milan, 1995.

BRIAN HORTON

I haven't argued with the manager over this, but I don't think it takes a scientist to work out that if a team gets beat 5-0, it's a bit strange if the centre-forward takes the bulk of the criticism.

> NIALL QUINN, Manchester City striker, on life with Horton, 1995.

KEVIN KEEGAN

If Kevin Keegan fell into the Tyne, he'd come up with a salmon in his mouth.

> JACK CHARLTON, Republic of Ireland manager, 1995.

He's a desperately bad loser. He needs to win all the time. If you're two steps behind Kevin Keegan, you'll not go far wrong.

> BARRY VENISON, Southampton midfielder and
> former Newcastle captain, 1995.

He is desperate to win every time, whether it's the FA Cup final or a game of head tennis.

> BRIAN KILCLINE, Newcastle defender, 1994.

For the first time since I became leader, my children were impressed by something I did. 'Did you really meet Kevin Keegan, dad?' 'Did you really do 27 consecutive headers?'

TONY BLAIR MP, Labour leader and Newcastle fan, after sharing a
photo opportunity with Keegan at the party conference, 1995.

HOWARD KENDALL

If I made a mistake at Notts County it was probably to mention publicly that I'd never been sacked in my life. I think the chairman wanted to say he spoiled my record.

KENDALL, former Everton and Manchester City manager, on being sacked
by Notts chairman Derek Pavis after 79 days, 1995.

JOE KINNEAR

I'm out at the moment, but should you be the chairman of Barcelona, AC Milan or Real Madrid, I'll get straight back to you. The rest can wait.

KINNEAR, Wimbledon manager, answer-phone message, 1995.

JOHN LAMBIE

We've argued all our working life. I've thrown him out of my car and I've thrown him out of his own house. But I like to think the arguments have been for the better of the business.

GEORGE FULSTON, Falkirk chairman, 1995.

BRIAN LITTLE

Everybody has faults and his is probably that he's not demonstrative enough.

DOUG ELLIS, Aston Villa chairman, on his manager, 1995.

When things went wrong (during my first season with Villa), I kept reminding myself of all the things I've done in football. I would say to myself: 'You have got this far, what have you done wrong?' And I kept answering: 'Not a lot'.

LITTLE on first anniversary as Villa manager, 1995.

After I joined Celtic I was walking down a street in Glasgow when someone shouted: 'Fenian bastard'. I had to go and look it up – Fenian, that is.

MICK McCARTHY, Yorkshire-born Republic of Ireland manager, 1996

MICK MCCARTHY

People seem to think that Jack Charlton and me are exactly the same. But I was a forthright, blunt, arrogant bastard long before I ever got involved with him.

McCARTHY, shortly before succeeding Charlton as
Republic of Ireland manager, 1995.

MARK MCGHEE

He's fat, he's round, he's taken Leicester down.

READING FANS' SONG aimed at their club's former manager, 1995.

I am fat. It's difficult not to get that way with the kind of life I lead, but the important thing is that it doesn't affect my golf swing.

McGHEE, then Leicester manager, responding to the taunts, 1995.

BORA MILUTINOVIC

Bora is a perfectionist. If he was married to Demi Moore, he'd expect her to be a good cook.

RICK DAVIS, US-TV summariser on the United States manager, 1994.

DAVID PLEAT

As the last man still sporting a quiff in Great Britain, David is used to things going a bit flat after a promising start.

JIMMY GREAVES as Sheffield Wednesday dropped down the Premiership, 1995.

BRUCE RIOCH

What I learned (in Seattle) were the Americans' positive attitudes – making people feel bright every day. I have tried to use that at all my clubs. If you ask people how they are, 95 per cent of them will say: 'Not bad'. Well no one says 'not bad' at Bolton. The response at this club is: 'Brilliant'. If people feel bad I don't want to know. I didn't get up in the morning to hear their problems.

RIOCH, then Bolton manager, 1994.

BRYAN ROBSON

His strengths as a manager are the same as they were as a player. He is single-minded, stubborn even, very determined. He is also very thorough. I went to see him before Middlesbrough's Coca-Cola Cup game against Palace, and he was in his little room, surrounded by all his data on them.

ALEX FERGUSON, Manchester United manager, on his former captain, 1995.

JOHN RUDGE

We all dread a phone call from John Rudge with his 'I've got no money, what've you got, I fancy this one' routine. Eventually he gets a cheap player and makes him into an even better player. Every game I go to, he's there with that 'bonnet' on, and that's dedication. Port Vale should go down on their knees and thank the Lord for having him.

ALEX FERGUSON, Manchester United manager, on the long-serving Port Vale manager, 1995.

GRAEME SOUNESS

He came in raging about a tackle by Denis Wise on Nigel Clough. In the end I had to tell him: 'Calm down, you've just had a triple heart by-pass'.

KEITH HACKETT, Sheffield referee, 1994.

It is not a case of me going because of the money. Football is the most important thing to me.

SOUNESS, former Rangers and Liverpool manager, on taking up a lucrative post with
Galatasaray in Turkey, 1995.

ALAN SMITH

It's no good me walking out. I'm not Kevin Keegan. They would not come rushing to the gates and drag me back. They would push me through them.

ALAN SMITH, Crystal Palace manager, as a feud with
chairman Ron Noades boiled and relegation loomed, 1995.

I might be a blazer and tie man and know how to use a knife and fork. But I will get down with the rats and fight to keep Palace in the Premiership. That will be my only satisfaction.

SMITH, 1995.

He won a title, got the club to the Coca-Cola semi-final and then the FA Cup semi-final. They would have had a statue built of him at most clubs.

ANONYMOUS PALACE PLAYER on Smith's departure, 1995.

WALTER SMITH

I didn't know Walter personally. But I knew he must be Scottish because I used to see him carrying big discount cases of lager back from the supermarket.

PAUL GASCOIGNE on his first meeting with his future manager at Rangers in Florida, 1995.

GRAHAM TAYLOR

Napoleon wanted his generals to be lucky. I don't think he would have wanted me.

TAYLOR, England manager, after elimination from the World Cup, 1993.

I can do other things. I wrote for *The Times* quite successfully. People seemed to think they were quite good articles, and they were easy to do.

TAYLOR in his final weeks with England, 1993.

John Major is the Graham Taylor of politics.

JOHN SMITH MP Leader of the Labour Party, 1993.

If a journalist wrote that about me he'd have to go into hiding.

JACK CHARLTON, Republic of Ireland manager, on the *Sun's* 'Turnip' jibe, 1993.

I used to quite like turnips. Now my wife refuses to serve them.

TAYLOR, between jobs, 1994.

I've never had a problem with the vegetable thing. There are a lot worse things to be called.

TAYLOR on taking over as Wolves manager, 1994.

I produced some of the best football I ever played (at Glasgow Rangers) and scored 29, 30 and 27 goals in consecutive seasons. Yet I never really got the credit I thought I deserved in England. I'm afraid that was down to Dick Turpin – I mean Graham Taylor. I got one game and that was it. If he'd played me more he might have kept his job.

MARK HATELEY, QPR striker, 1995.

You can call him a hornet, but don't call him a turnip.

> ELTON JOHN, Watford life president and former chairman,
> on Taylor's return to the club, 1996.

Being an ex-England manager, one that failed to qualify for the World Cup, is like being a dead politician.

> TAYLOR, back at Watford, 1996.

TERRY VENABLES

Spurs without Terry is like Westminster without Big Ben.

> PAUL GASCOIGNE reacting to Venables' sacking by Alan Sugar, 1993.

I feel like Robin Hood – feared by the bad, loved by the good.

> VENABLES on his dismissal by Sugar.

There are many who would like to see Venables as England's manager, but he has this funny reputation.

> SIR BERT MILLICHIP, chairman of the FA, 1994.

I would like Venables installed before the European Championship draw in Manchester at the weekend. It would be a marvellous publicity stunt if he were there.

> MILLICHIP three days later.

I must be the only person who could actually get less publicity by becoming manager of England.

> VENABLES, newly appointed England coach, on continuing controversy
> surrounding his business dealings, 1994.

I do not accept his evidence as entirely reliable, to put it at its most charitable.

> MR RECORDER WILLIAMS, giving judgement against Venables' nightclub,
> Scribes West, over an unpaid bill, 1995.

The Spurs players with England don't consider ourselves Terry's mates. We are his players. But what's wrong with having a drink with the manager and getting to know each other? It doesn't mean we're getting shit-faced at Scribes every night.

> TEDDY SHERINGHAM, Tottenham and England striker, 1995.

People say I have my favourites. That's bullshit. I've got a big job. I've got favourite people for playing football, no other reason.

VENABLES on the continued absence of Matthew Le Tissier
from the national squad, 1995.

Sometimes a manager will say something and you'll think: 'Well, I don't know about that'. But with him you think: 'Yeah'. Whenever I go back to him now, I learn something. And being a nice man, he makes you want to play for him.

DARREN ANDERTON, Tottenham and England midfielder, 1995.

Once we're away (on holiday) he switches off, but he obviously still thinks about what he's going to do because he doodles England attack plans on napkins. I get up in the morning and all the newspapers are covered in crosses and arrows.

YVETTE VENABLES, wife, 1995.

(At Barcelona) there were all these women baking him cakes, knitting him jumpers and sending rude pictures of themselves. But I don't worry – he's definitely a man's man, happier in men's company than women's.

YVETTE VENABLES, 1995.

His hobby is watching football videos – he's just so dedicated to it that he watches videos in his spare time to find out what goes on in other countries. He's studying certain teams at the moment and once he gets into that he's mesmerised – he just sits like a child in front of a cartoon. He's totally devoted to it. It's his life.

YVETTE VENABLES, 1995.

He's a great tactician, the best in the country and respected throughout the world for it, which is something I admire because I don't do tactics.

BARRY FRY, Birmingham manager, 1995.

I was going to ask him what he thought my idea for a Terry Venables theme nightclub called Wormwood Scribes, but chickened out.

FRANK SKINNER, comedian, on meeting the England coach, 1996.

BERTI VOGTS

If people saw me walking on water you can be sure someone would say: 'Look at that Berti Vogts, he can't even swim'.

VOGTS, Germany coach, 1996.

NEIL WARNOCK

I've had to do dirty deeds wherever I've been. Clubs only send for me when they're in trouble, so there's usually some unpleasant business to sort out before you hit the straight and narrow.

WARNOCK, Huddersfield manager, 1995.

RAY WILKINS

Ray's been at clubs like Milan where you have to wear a suit to bed, so he's very strict about the dress code.

DANIELE DICHIO, QPR striker, 1995.

HOWARD WILKINSON

He disliked personalities who had a rapport with the fans.

ERIC CANTONA, former Leeds striker, in *Cantona: My Story*, 1994.

If I'm ever reincarnated, I'd like to return as a personality.

WILKINSON, Leeds manager, 1995.

For all the problems Cantona has had since leaving us, he was never in bother during his time at Leeds. That shows the quality of management here.

LESLIE SILVER, Leeds chairman, after Cantona's dismissal and fracas with a spectator at Crystal Palace, 1995.

CHAPTER 4
The Beautiful Game

Style

The most beautiful game is winning matches.

GLENN HODDLE, Chelsea manager, 1995.

Thank you for letting me play in your beautiful football.

ERIC CANTONA accepting the PFA Player of the Year award, 1994.

I love the speed of the game here. Playing from goal to goal, keeping the momentum going at all times. There's beauty in the game here. The spontaneity is beautiful.

CANTONA, from *La Philosophie de Cantona*, 1995.

See the boy Rudyard Kipling, who said it wasn't whether you won but how you played the game that mattered, well he obviously never played football. Winning is the only thing that matters.

ANDY GORAM, Rangers and Scotland goalkeeper, 1996.

When the Queen came to the Bahamas, I told her – and football is not her favourite pastime – 'Maam, you must realise that people live for this game'.

SIR JACK HAYWARD, Bahamas-based Wolves owner and president, 1994.

It is the greatest game in the world. It is also the most frustrating, exasperating, infuriating, desolating game. But there is nothing else.

KEN BATES, Chelsea chairman, 1995.

It was enthralling. I'd been to rugger matches but never seen Association Football live. One just had no idea of the speed these men operate at.

COUNTESS OF ELGIN on her first soccer match, Celtic v Motherwell, 1995.

Football is a saving grace. I know it's a very flippant thing to say, but if Kurt Cobain (Nirvana singer who committed suicide) had played football, he'd probably still be alive today. If you play football, you'll know what that means. Football has given me the simplicity that I'm always trying to find...I find it increasingly hard to find things that it can't solve. To do with love, maybe. It doesn't solve anything between men and women, but I think it can solve most things between men and men.

DAMON ALBARN, singer with the pop group Blur and a Chelsea fan,
in *New Musical Express*, 1995.

Q: What does English football mean to you?
A: English football is fundamentally different to anywhere else. It's given me a lot more than I've given it.

ERIC CANTONA in interview with French press, 1994.

I love to listen to the football results and the lulling rollcall of team names – Sheffield Wednesday, West Bromwich Albion, Partick Thistle, Queen of the South; what glory there is in those names – and I find strange comfort in the exotic and mystifying litany of the shipping forecasts. I have no idea what they mean – 'Viking rising five, backing four; Dogger blowing strong, steady as she goes; Minches gale force 12, jeez Louise' – but they exert a powerful and soothing effect on me. I genuinely believe that one of the reasons Britain is such a steady and gracious place is the calming influence of the football results and shipping forecasts.

BILL BRYSON, American travel writer, on his adopted country
in *Notes From A Small Island*, 1995.

I finish games and come off the pitch not wanting the referee to have blown the whistle because I'm enjoying myself so much. Can you believe that? We might be winning only 1-0 and all I want to do is carry on playing. Every Sunday I sit in the dressing-room and feel real disappointment that I have to wait another week to get out there again.

DAVID PLATT, England captain, on playing for Sampdoria, 1994.

There are not many here (England) I would consider for Italy. But all of those in Italy could play in England. I am not joking – all of them. The best and most important football is played in Italy.

RUUD GULLIT, Chelsea's former Milan and Sampdoria player, 1995.

Everybody talks about how good the foreign players are – how great their touch is, how much skill they've got, their marvellous aware-ness – but very few seem to appreciate their fitness. You don't see an unfit European side. You don't see their players fat and bloated. They're all gaunt and look like athletes.

MIKE WALKER, Everton manager, 1994.

Football is like a car. You've got five gears, but the trouble with Eng-lish teams is that they drive in fourth and fifth all the time. They never use first, second and third, never build up as you should. When they crash in Europe they say it's bad luck. It isn't – it's bad driving.

RUUD GULLIT on joining Chelsea, 1995.

England will never win World Cups. We simply don't have enough people who believe in playing football.

ALEX FERGUSON, Manchester United manager (and a Scot), 1995.

When English sides play in Europe, their opponents still know what is coming: the long ball into the penalty area, which gets nowhere; the next ball, which the opposition win; and the counter-attack, which English clubs cannot deal with.

ANTONIO PACHECO, Portugal player, 1995.

When Greeks learn the game, we concentrate on keeping the ball on the ground. We like football you can watch on one television, not played so long and high that you need to stack up the TV sets to watch it.

ALEXIS DEDES, Greece manager, in Scotland for
European Championship qualifier, 1995.

Hump it, bump it, whack it might be one possible recipe for a good sex life, but it won't win us the World Cup.

> KEN BATES, Chelsea chairman, after England's elimination
> under Graham Taylor, 1993.

This is not the Italian League, or the German, or the Dutch, or Spanish or French or English leagues. This is the Irish League and it is different. If a player comes over here from England and tries to put his foot on the ball, show a bit of skill in midfield, he gets hit by a bus. And if he misses the first bus, there's a second bus coming along and that will kill him.

> BOBBY BAXTER, Monaghan manager, 1994.

I'd like to see a bit more skill and less humping it towards the corner flags. We're the best league at hitting the corner flags in the world.

> BOBBY BAXTER, 1994

The problem is that Thatcherite Premier League. They're breeding greed. Eventually they get found out, and they're being found out now.

> TERRY YORATH, Wales manager, after elimination of his team
> and England from the World Cup, 1993.

The clubs get a lot of TV money now, but what are they doing with it? They're getting three times the money but they're just paying the players three times as much. And the players aren't getting better. We've got to invest in coaching and youngsters. We've been anti-coaching for so many years. That's why the game has passed us by — because we don't reach for perfection.

> TERRY VENABLES, England coach, after watching Ajax, 1996.

I'd be the ruination of the game if I got my way. All I want to see is goalies keeping clean sheets. That's not what the fans want, is it?

> ALAN HODGKINSON, former England keeper and Scotland goalkeeping coach, 1996.

We went out and played the Ajax system — three at the back, three in midfield, three up front, and a pair of rosary beads for Christy McElligott in goal.

> BRIAN KERR, manager of St Patrick's Athletic, Dublin,
> on his tactics after his keeper was sent off, 1995.

There was a lot of space out there, but all the players abused it.

DAVID PLEAT, Sheffield Wednesday manager, after 0-0 draw with Chelsea, 1995.

A 0-0 draw in Italy is crap. In England, a 0-0 draw can be really interesting.

IAN WRIGHT, Arsenal and England striker, 1995.

Where are the George Bests of English football?

NILS ARNE EGGEN, coach to Rosenborg Trondheim of Norway,
after beating Blackburn, 1995.

I originally called my midfield 'Dogs of War', half-jokingly. People don't realise how much the game has changed in midfield over the years. The playmaker who stands on the ball and sprays it everywhere after five pints and a cigar in the pub simply doesn't exist any more.

JOE ROYLE, Everton manager, 1995.

The World Cup wasn't won on the playing fields of England, it was won on the streets.

SIR BOBBY CHARLTON, member of the victorious England side, 1995.

I can appreciate that the game has got quicker and more physical – because of teams pushing up and squeezing the play – (but) I don't think the quality of the players has improved. The players of my generation learned the basic ball skills as small boys, practising in the street. The hunger to master the ball isn't there any more. Because of the way the game's gone, tactically, it hasn't been necessary anyway.

ALAN BALL, Southampton manager, 1995.

I was right-footed to start with but I worked harder on my left and it became better than my right. It annoys me today when I see players earning £20,000 a week who can't kick with both feet. I find it amazing that professionals can't do that.

GEORGE BEST, in TV interview with Michael Parkinson on 50th birthday, 1996.

There are those going to games now in Scotland who have never watched what I consider to be good football. We have players in this country who are regarded as heroes but cannot, in my opinion, play football at all.

ERNIE WALKER, former secretary to the Scottish FA, 1995.

To be honest I'd prefer the Irish style at Leeds and less of that over-lapping.

GARY KELLY after winning accolades for his display v Portugal, 1995.

There was one player at Tottenham, and I name no names, who couldn't pass the ball to a white shirt. It looks to you like I'm exaggerating, but in a proper game, under pressure, controlling the ball was not easy for him.

OSSIE ARDILES, former Tottenham manager, 1995.

When I read about some player being a hard worker, I just don't want to know. A professional shouldn't be anything else but fit, so there's no hard work in just being able to run. The hard work comes when you have to play with imagination.

IVAN GOLAC, Dundee United manager, 1994.

We came and joined the party, we didn't spoil it.

ALAN BALL, Southampton manager, after defeat at Anfield when
Liverpool paraded the Coca-Cola Cup, 1995.

I spent 45 minutes after the game telling them that they lacked endeavour and passion for the shirt. But I didn't get any reaction. You never do when they know they're in the wrong. Players hide behind every excuse in the book...Players of today aren't facing up to their responsibilities in return for their salaries and adulation.

BALL, by now Manchester City manager, after defeat at QPR, 1995.

Any player not inspired by that atmosphere should go and play golf with his grandmother.

CLEMENS WESTERHOF, Nigeria coach, at the Foxboro Stadium,
near Boston, World Cup finals, 1994.

I'd shoot myself if I had the bottle.

VINNIE JONES, Wimbledon midfielder, after being sent off
for the 10th time, 1995.

I'd hang myself but we can't afford the rope.

IAIN MUNRO, Hamilton Academical manager, 1995.

Nobody ever won a tackle with a smile on his face.

BRUCE RIOCH, Bolton manager, 1994.

My father gave me standards and yet I stepped out of them when I played. You could say it was the spirit of the time, the law of the jungle, but then you look at Bobby Charlton and realise that was no excuse. It was down to your own temperament and the guidance you were given by managers and coaches. That's why I wouldn't countenance, from my players, some of the things I did.

RIOCH, 1995.

I stepped forward and I collided with (John) McStay. Subsequently he fell to the ground.

DUNCAN FERGUSON, Everton striker, giving evidence on his appeal against conviction for assault while playing for Rangers, 1995.

I am very disappointed that a young man who has a job and is no danger to society has been sent to prison.

PETER JOHNSON, Everton chairman, on Ferguson's prison sentence, 1995.

It is the first time I have seen players from the same team fighting. It was a very strange situation.

JIM HANSEN, Uefa observer at the Spartak Moscow – Blackburn match, 1995.

Monster, Monster shocked.

ERIC HALL, agent, reacting to Dennis Wise's three-month jail sentence for assault, 1995.

Monster, Monster happy.

HALL on hearing Wise's sentence was suspended.

The FA have given me a pat on the back. I've taken violence off the terracing and on to the pitch.

VINNIE JONES, Wimbledon midfielder, speaking to the Oxford Union, 1995.

I don't want my players behaving like poofters – I want them to be men.

DAVE BASSETT, Sheffield United manager, after his player Tom Cowan was accused of overreacting to a push by Roy Keane, 1993.

It's becoming a game for fairies.

KEITH BURKINSHAW, West Bromwich Albion manager, 1994.

The pitch was playable. I've been in football over 25 years and it's become a game for poofters.

JOHN BURRIDGE, Manchester City goalkeeper, after game was postponed, 1995.

Can I point out that the gay Stonewall Football Club's third XI played a West End League fixture on a Somme-like Regent's Park afternoon on Sunday, therefore challenging (Burridge's) theory that a player's sexual orientation has any connection with getting muddy knees.

LETTER from Stonewall FC to *The Independent*, 1995.

If you played soccer at school in Canberra, you were looked on as a right poofter.

ANDY BERNAL, Reading's Australian defender, 1996.

My conscience is clear. I always put my hand on my groin when I'm warming up.

EDMUNDO, Flamengo striker rebutting charges that he had made an obscene gesture to Vasco da Gama fans, 1995.

It's the collective part of the team which is important. If I'd wanted to draw attention to myself I'd have played singles tennis, or chosen a nice lady for mixed doubles.

ERIC CANTONA, 1993.

Of course I wasn't nervous. Taking a penalty to win the Cup is what you are in the game for. If you don't feel excited by that, perhaps you should not be a professional footballer.

CANTONA, on his two penalties in the FA Cup fina
which gave United the Double, 1994.

I know only one way to take penalties: to score them.

CANTONA, from *La Philosophie de Cantona*, 1995.

I asked the players who wanted to take a penalty, and there was an awful smell coming from a few of them.

MICK McCARTHY, Millwall manager, after penalty shoot-out win, 1995.

Maybe they should have given the money to a Third Division football team.

JEREMY ISAACS, director of the Royal Opera House, on criticism of a £55m
award from the National Lottery, 1995.

I don't know of any other industry that would lay out £8.5m on anything and then not have some plan from day one on how they're going to use it.

STAN COLLYMORE, Britain's record buy, as Liverpool struggled
to integrate him into the team, 1995.

When Tottenham Hotspur breaks the rules, it gets fined £1.5m. What's good for the goose is good for the sauerkraut.

TOTTENHAM SPOKESMAN justifying protest to Uefa over Bayern Munich's
approach to Jurgen Klinsmann, 1995.

Players should have the same rights as other workers, like anyone else on my staff. The only things that are going to save football will be sponsorship and television rights. I can't quadruple ticket prices in my area.

SIR JOHN HALL, Newcastle chairman, on the Bosman ruling, 1995.

Football is bankrupt without the TV deals. If the banks ever withdrew, you'd see a collapse bigger than Black Monday.

SIR JOHN HALL, 1995.

Either you sort it out or you have five clubs with cheque books battling it out and 15 others providing cannon fodder.

ALAN SUGAR, Tottenham chairman, after the Bergkamp
and Collymore deals, 1995.

There are no bungs in football. With my so-called reputation, I would be the one they approached. I deal with most clubs, most managers, and I've never been asked for a bung or offered one. A fact.

ERIC HALL, agent, 1995.

Our biggest concern is there is a growing perception the game is riddled with corruption. All of us involved in it know that is simply not the case.

BRENDAN BATSON, players union official, after the bung
and bribe scandals, 1995.

Maybe I'm naive (about match-fixing allegations), but I just can't believe all this is happening. Everybody knows how seriously we (goalkeepers) take our job...The sound of the ball hitting the net – the old death rattle, I call it – is the worst sound in the world to me...In training today, one of our reserve keepers was saying he felt tired after playing twice in two days. I actually said that if he didn't show a better attitude, I'd smash him in the flipping face. That's what keeping the ball out of the net means to me.

JOHN BURRIDGE, 43-year-old 'freelance' keeper, 1995.

I play every game to win. I go out to die for my team. If I knew I was playing with a crooked team-mate, someone not with us, then someone else would have to die. Me fix a game? There's more chance of me being involved with the Great Train Robbery.

VINNIE JONES, Wimbledon captain, after arrest
of team-mate Hans Segers, 1995.

I expect to see people walking down the streets of every major city now, kicking balls when they should be going to work. It's going to be great.

PRESIDENT BILL CLINTON in phone message to United States squad
at start of World Cup finals, 1994.

This was like taking the first two sips of Dom Perignon, two bites of the first ripe tomatoes of midsummer, two licks of chocolate ice-cream at Tre Scarlini in Rome. It was what the French call amusè-juèlè, something to tantalise the palate.

CHICAGO TRIBUNE report on Brazil's victory over Russia
at World Cup finals, 1994.

Soccer is certainly gaining ground with me. If I could live for a thousand years, I'd now set aside a decade for soccer. Before this World Cup began, I'd have given soccer about the same time slot in eternity as auto racing: maybe a week.

THOMAS BOSWELL, sportswriter and baseball afficionado,
in Washington Post, 1994.

All that (soccer's popularity around the world) proves is that most of the world is too poor to build bowling alleys, golf courses, tennis courts and baseball fields. There's hundreds of millions of poor people out there who still ain't got indoor plumbing, but that don't mean there's something great about an outhouse. Soccer is boring. I've never seen a more boring sport.

MIKE ROYKO, columnist, Detroit Free Press, 1994.

Soccer will never take over from baseball. Baseball's the only chance we blacks get to wave a bat at a white man without starting a riot.

EDDIE MURPHY, actor, during World Cup finals, 1994.

That's why most foreigners are shorter than Americans. All those balls bouncing off their heads compress their necks and spines.

ROYKO, writing in the Chicago Tribune during World Cup finals, 1994.

Another episode of Soccer in the Sauna.

RON NEWMAN, American TV pundit, as Germany v South Korea
began in a temperature of over 120 in Dallas, 1994.

Beating Argentina is the greatest moment for our people since the revolution.

ANGHEL IORDANESCU, Romania coach, 1994.

Soccer is cruel, fate is relentless and the most coveted championship in the world hinged on the caprice of a leather boot striking a leather ball on a chalk spot 12 yards from a goal.

LOS ANGELES TIMES after goalless World Cup final was settled on penalties, 1994.

126 Million Seconds to France '98

HEADLINE in Soccer Canada magazine at end of World Cup finals, 1994.

Some journalist wrote that 'There are some people on the pitch... They think it's all over...It is now!' ranked with Winston Churchill when he said 'Never in the field of human conflict', but that may be going a bit far.

KENNETH WOLSTENHOLME, former BBC-TV commentator, 1995.

I know how long it takes a goat to die once it has had its throat cut.

BARRY VENISON, Southampton defender, on what he had learnt in
his spell with Turkish club Galatasaray, 1995.

When I made my debut for Besiktas they even sacrificed a lamb, which is a sacred animal, on the pitch. Its blood was then daubed on my forehead and boots to bring me good luck. They never did that at QPR.

LES FERDINAND, Newcastle striker, on his spell in Turkey, 1995.

It's a question of to Hell and back.

BRIAN KIDD, Manchester United assistant manager,
on returning to Istanbul, 1994.

Anyone who thinks these things don't happen is living in cloud cuckoo land.

GRAHAM TAYLOR, former England manager, on his liberal use of foul language
during the Channel 4 documentary, *Cutting Edge*, 1994.

To people in Spain, the FA Cup is all about Wembley, sunshine and great teams. But we don't see the matches like this on muddy, sloping pitches, in cold and wet conditions with professionals playing part-timers.

ROBERTO MARTINEZ, Wigan Athletic player, after draw at Runcorn, 1995.

It wasn't much fun letting in four, five or six goals every week. That's basically what it was. I can't stand there and take stick for that week in, week out. Enough is enough.

MARC OSBOURNE, Albion Rovers goalkeeper, on why he failed to turn up for a
match v Queen's Park, 1995. Rovers played a striker in goal and lost 4-0.

My dad rang me from Vancouver. He thought there was a misprint on TV.

CRAIG FORREST, Ipswich's Canadian goalkeeper, after 9-0
defeat by Manchester United, 1995.

I'd love to be still going in my late thirties, like Bryan Robson, but I doubt that I will be. The game's still getting faster and I reckon the retirement age will be down to about 32 in another 10 years.

STEVE MCMANAMAN, Liverpool and England winger, 1995.

When I wake up in the morning and get a burning feeling in my ears I usually know that I'm going to play well.

MICHAEL PREUD'HOMME, Belgium goalkeeper, 1994.

People think football is a game, but it's a limited company, a business.

IAN BRANFOOT, Southampton manager.

I couldn't live without football. I can never understand players who say they want to retire at the top. It's the same game whether you're playing for Real Madrid or the Scott Lithgow Shipyard Second XI. I'd have been playing until I was 50 if I'd been all right.

ALLAN McGRAW, Greenock Morton manager, disabled by injuries, 1995.

Furniture polish is so important – it gives you so much more control over the player.

DARREN CLARK, British Subbuteo champion, on the International Federation's threat to ban players putting furniture polish on the figures' bases, 1994.

Just when I thought it was safe to go to parties again and say I was a footballer.

GARRY NELSON, Charlton striker, in *Left Foot Forward: Diary of a Journeyman Footballer*, on Eric Cantona's leap into the Selhurst Park crowd, 1995.

Lifestyle

Footballers are only interested in drinking, clothes and the size of their willies.

KARREN BRADY, Birmingham City managing director, 1994.

At first when I did a tour of the changing rooms, I sent someone ahead to check if any of the players were visible. When I entered, they were waiting for me, all completely nude with a smile on their lips.

BRADY, 1995.

We thought we'd find that footballers have an extremely hard life. Pressure from the crowds and referees, TV cameras on them all the time, and the general inspection of their lifestyle led us to expect that they suffered enormous levels of stress. But that wasn't the case.

DR HOWARD KAHN, psychology lecturer, Heriot-Watt University,
announcing findings of interviews with 500 Scottish professionals, 1996..

Professionalism (in rugby) implies a soccer-style mentality, training in the morning and reading comics in the afternoon.

ED GRIFFITHS, South African Rugby Union chief executive, 1995.

The Boss is away today, so as the old saying goes: 'When the cat is away, the mice go running'.

BRIAN McCLAIR, on training at Manchester United,
in 'Choccy's Soccer Diary', *United Magazine*, 1996.

I never wanted to be a coach because I've a low opinion of players. Footballers are the most obnoxious, ignorant and selfish people.

EDWIN STEIN, Birmingham coach, 1993.

Q: What's the worst thing anyone's ever said to you?
A: You're not playing.

MARK STEIN, Chelsea striker and brother of Edwin,
in *Sun* questionnaire, 1995.

I was slaughtered for reading *The Guardian*. In most walks of life, that would be respected, differences valued. Because of the way lads are, it came out the other way. I took the stick but wasn't very happy and quite often it was upsetting. But I stuck it out when I had plenty of opportunities to fit in with the sheep.

GRAEME LE SAUX, Blackburn and England defender, 1995.

It's a good dressing-room to be in. They'll talk about Bosnia, politics, world issues, everything.

DAVID PLATT, England captain, on life in Italy with Sampdoria, 1995.

You go into a shop and it's just Armani this and that, and you buy it. Clothes that you don't even need. I spent a grand once. Bit of a waste really.

GARY KELLY, Leeds and Republic of Ireland defender, 1995.

I've no doubt that Alan Shearer's salary would make an ideal minimum for everyone.

GORDON TAYLOR, chief executive to Professional Footballers' Association, addressing the Trades Union Congress, 1995.

Very few players can really play well when they're earning a lot of money. They find it harder to be motivated when all the bills are being paid and when they're sure of having a holiday and a new car every year.

MARK McGHEE, Wolves manager, 1996.

Money is not a criteria for some people. There are multi-millionaires who still get up at 6am to get going about their business. They are winners. For players it doesn't matter what bonus they are on, playing is the meat and drink and winning is the bonus. It's the winning that gives them the kicks.

ALEX FERGUSON, Manchester United manager, 1995.

They need to want to be better but some of the players think: 'I've got a million in the bank, why bother to work harder?'

RAY HARFORD, Blackburn manager, during champions' poor start to season, 1995.

I USUALLY GO OUT AFTER A GAME WEARING A NORMAL SUIT –
ARMANI, VERSACE, THE SAME AS WHAT MOST OF THE LADS
WEAR.

DAVID JAMES, Liverpool goalkeeper and fashion model, 1996.

People will say that I've got a screw loose, that I've lost it, but perhaps it's just that I'm in the 0.1 per cent of footballers who don't give a toss about unlimited money.

MATTHEW LE TISSIER, Southampton midfielder, on why he had stayed loyal to the club, 1995.

Footballers have to say that money doesn't matter. If they say it does matter they know it'll be spread all over the press – 'greedy, overpaid players etc'.

JOHN BARNES, Liverpool and England midfielder, 1995.

Does anybody in their right mind think David Platt has come over here for wages? Does anybody think Bergkamp has come here for wages?...I laugh when I read Bergkamp is on this or Jurgen Klinsmann is on that. They are not over here for salaries, they get a fee and then they get a salary. Or they don't come.

GEORGE GRAHAM, former Arsenal manager, in *The Glory and the Grief*, 1995.

People have been laying the blame at my door for everything, from the washing machine breaking down to me supposedly demanding half a million pounds each week.

STEVE CLARIDGE, Leicester striker, on his rancorous parting with Birmingham, 1996.

I wince at players who cheat and foul, who abuse referees and who think only about winning and the money it will bring.

TONY BLAIR MP leader of the Labour Party, on the modern game, 1995.

I wouldn't give up football even if I won the £18m jackpot on the National Lottery. I love this job and I'd even pay to play rather than not play at all.

DEAN HOLDSWORTH, Wimbledon striker, 1995.

As a footballer you can be playing away happily, your children can be doing well at school and your wife can be settled, but none of that matters. If the manager wants rid of you, he can make life very difficult until you agree to go.

MARK McGHEE, Wolves manager, recalling the insecurity of his playing career, 1996.

Nothing scares me in football. I'm the same at home – the bills come in left, right and centre, but I never look at them until the red ones arrive.

STEVE STONE, Nottingham Forest and England midfielder, 1995.

I've taken a pay cut to come here. As long as the fridge is full, I'm happy.

GORDON STRACHAN, Coventry assistant manager, on leaving Leeds, 1995.

One of my favourite snacks is a big can of mushy peas topped with mint sauce. Trev (Trevor Lea, Manchester United nutritionist) says it's a great source of protein – so I have four cans a week.

RYAN GIGGS, 1995.

There was no magic formula (for getting in shape). I just went running four miles up the Heswall Hills every night and kept off the Kentucky Fried Chicken.

JOHN BARNES, newly slimmed-down Liverpool midfielder, 1995.

Favourite food: Fish and chips. I don't like any of that Indian, Italian or Chinese stuff.

CHRIS JACKSON, Barnsley striker, in club programme's 'Personal File', 1995.

Sometimes I'd have to go next door to get fed. I've seen people starving and I know that side of life.

DWIGHT YORKE, Aston Villa striker, on his impoverished childhood in Tobago, 1996.

There are one or two players about who'd like the competition renamed the Vodka and Coca-Cola Cup.

RON ATKINSON, Aston Villa manager, before the final, 1994.

All the great players I've ever known enjoyed a good drink.

JIM BAXTER, former Scotland midfielder, 1993.

In my experience it is usually the legendary drinkers at a club who are the best trainers. Okay, they go out and get into an unathletic state but, come the next training day, they put in more effort than the non-drinkers because they feel they have to.

JOHN COLQUHOUN, Hearts and former Scotland striker,
in his *Scotland on Sunday* column. 1996.

I was so certain the game would be off that I went out on Friday night and got full of Bacardi.

> DAMIAN BRAY, Burntisland Shipyard defender, after 7-0 defeat by Huntly,
> Scottish Cup, 1995. Huntly had cleared 40 tons of snow from the pitch
> to enable the game to go ahead.

It was a big surprise to me at Ipswich to see how much the players would drink. In Kiev, if you arrived for training with red eyes, smelling or without sleep, no one would speak to you because they felt you had let the side down.

> SERGEI BALTACHA, former Dynamo Kiev, Ipswich and Soviet Union
> player shortly after leaving manager's post at Caledonian Thistle, 1995.

Q: Who has been the biggest influence on your career?
A: IAN ST JOHN: Bill Shankly.
A: JIMMY GREAVES: Vladimir Smirnoff.

> INTERVIEW with Saint and Greavsie in *Loaded* magazine, 1995.

Now it's a gallon or two of cold lager, a day to recover and back to the building site at 7 o'clock on Monday morning.

> CHRIS BRINDLEY, Kidderminster centre-half,
> after FA Cup win at Birmingham, 1994.

Our players don't bloody drink for a start. There are no 12-pints-a-night men here. They go straight home to their families and always behave like responsible athletes.

> BOBBY ROBSON, Porto manager, explaining why Portuguese clubs
> are doing better than English ones in European competition, 1995.

Glasgow's an incredible city for rumours. One minute I was supposedly negotiating with Rangers, the next I was out until six in the morning.

> PAUL ELLIOTT, former Celtic midfielder, 1995.

I never went to Stringfellows that much. I preferred Tramp.

> CHARLIE NICHOLAS, Celtic midfielder, on the Eighties high life in London, 1995.

Cocaine is the footballer's drug. It's expensive and glamorous with that champagne image, and its use is widespread among the top clubs.

> MARK DENNIS, former full-back, 1994.

I've heard that there are two well-known footballers – nothing to do with West Ham or Everton – who have not been caught and are heavily into 'social' drugs.

TONY COTTEE, West Ham and former Everton striker, 1995.

I took those pills as if they were aspirin. Thousands of players do it, but the cost is always higher for Maradona.

DIEGO MARADONA on his suspension for drug taking, World Cup finals, 1994.

There are times when I'm in a nightclub and people don't just come up to me and offer me drugs, they ask to buy them off me! They actually think I'm a dealer. I play for QPR, earn good money and they actually think I deal in drugs. Unbelievable.

TREVOR SINCLAIR, QPR striker, 1995.

I've had some bad days – three in eight months. If you go to the hairdressers five times, by the end of the week you're going to have a haircut. So I just avoid pubs. Every now and then I'll go in and have a coke. But it's a day-to-day thing. Tomorrow, who knows, it could be completely different.

PAUL MERSON, Arsenal midfielder, on fighting his alcoholism, 1995.

If it was a straight choice between having sex and scoring a goal, I'd go for the goal every time. I've got all my life to have sex.

ANDY GRAY, Sky summariser and former Scotland striker on *Danny Baker After All* BBC-TV show, 1995.

Gazza said recently that scoring a goal was better than an orgasm. Lee Chapman said it wasn't as good. I think I'll go with Pele – he thought it was about the same.

RYAN GIGGS, Manchester United winger, 1994.

Sex is one of the most relaxing things you can do, so they (players) should do it whenever they feel like it. The night before a game, the morning before a game, it doesn't matter as long as you don't do it during the game.

ERIC HALL, agent, 1995.

It's not the sex that tires out young players – it's staying up all night looking for it.

CLEMENS WESTERHOF, Dutch coach to Nigeria, World Cup finals, 1994.

FOWLER: I know someone who had a wank two hours before a game and went out and scored three.

McMANAMAN: I know him. He captains his country. But I think the no-sex thing is a load of shite really.

ROBBIE FOWLER and STEVE McMANAMAN in interview with Loaded magazine, 1995.

I went training once with £4,500 in my pocket and ran out of petrol on the way home because I'd spent the lot (betting on horses). I had to hitch a lift.

STEVE CLARIDGE, Leicester striker, confessing a gambling habit, 1996.

I like a bit of rough – footballers, roofers, blokes who get banged up.

DANNIELLA WESTBROOK, EastEnders actress, 1996.

I tend to buy family men. With a married player you generally know he is at home in the evening watching Coronation Street.

BRUCE RIOCH, Arsenal manager, 1995.

Sunday 31 July: I manage to venture out of the house to turn the sprinkler on the lawn and then on to the local garden centre with Chloe to see the ducks.

ALAN SHEARER, Blackburn and England striker, revealing all in Diary of a Season: The Inside Story of a Champion Year, 1995.

I do not envy those colleagues who must spend the winter reporting the doings of illiterate players and suspicious managers. What sort of world is it where Eric Cantona is an object of wonder because he reads second-rate French poets? Michael Atherton (England cricket captain) towers above him in intellect and – another thing altogether – intellectual discipline. Moreover, he doesn't wear a baseball cap back to front.

MICHAEL HENDERSON, Times cricket writer, in The Cricketer magazine, 1994.

Lots of footballers don't have a high IQ to start with, so it would be difficult to gauge the effects of heading the ball too much.

> JOHN COLQUHOUN, Hearts striker, on findings that alleged brain damage
> to players from heading, 1995.

I hate golf and I like architecture. I wouldn't say I go round looking at cathedrals but I do like old houses. I don't say a lot but I do think a lot, and that seems to surprise people who think all footballers are thick.

> BRIAN DEANE, Leeds striker, 1996.

My handicap is 16. I'm the only black man who can beat them – they don't want to be beaten by me.

> RUUD GULLIT, Chelsea midfielder, on playing golf with his team-mates, 1996.

Q: What films do you like?
A: Quentin Tarantino and stuff like that. There's nothing better than a good bit of violence!

> MARK DRAPER, Aston Villa midfielder, answering questions
> in *BigShots* magazine, 1995.

If it was left to the players' own devices they would have two weeks in Tenerife, followed by two weeks in Cyprus and another two in the pub.

> DAVID SULLIVAN, joint owner, Birmingham City, after allegations that
> the club's pre-season schedule was too gruelling, 1995.

When it's cold and raining I still remember that prison exercise yard and it makes me train that much harder.

> RICKY OTTO, Birmingham winger and former detainee
> at Her Majesty's Pleasure, 1995.

The food is terrible, the tea is like petrol and you get the usual stuff like people asking you to sign your autograph on a piece of toilet paper because they want to wipe their backside on it. And that's just the nice part.

> MICKEY THOMAS, former Wales midfielder, on life in prison, 1995.

You get turned over by the press now and again – it goes with the territory.

> DAVID PLATT, England captain, on his relationship with the media, 1995.

The press in Turkey are 10 times worse than they are here.

MIKE MARSH, Southend midfielder, recalling his brief spell with Galatasaray, 1995.

For the press, you're either brilliant or you're crap. We didn't win so it was crap. That's how they work.

TEDDY SHERINGHAM, Enland striker, after 0–0 draw v Croatia, 1996.

It was never like this at Stafford Rangers. I was lucky to get one interview every six months there.

STAN COLLYMORE on media demands after joining Liverpool, 1995.

Three or four of the lads here buy the quality papers. At Palace it was always eight *Suns*, four *Mirrors*.

GARETH SOUTHGATE, Aston Villa defender, on the reading habits at his present and former clubs, 1995.

I asked for a Valderrama and they gave me a Val Doonican.

ANDY TOWNSEND, Republic of Ireland captain, on unveiling new hairstyle during the World Cup finals, 1994.

'Start the season in style with Gazza' – cut and colour; 'Dutch Master' – Van Hooijdonk classic taper; or the 'Manchester Pose' – Giggs cut and perm.

SIGN in window of hairdressers' shop, Glasgow, 1995.

It seems one day you're gazing at pictures of top players in a sticker book, and then suddenly you're in the book yourself. It took me a long time to get used to it – perhaps longer than it should've done.

LES FERDINAND, Newcastle's £6m striker, 1995.

Q: Your worst nightmare?
A: To live in the East End or up North.

ANDREW IMPEY, QPR midfielder, in programme questionnaire, 1996.

The hardcore stereotypes are still there, but there are individuals in the game. Managers, players and supporters should accept and respect them for what they are. I have to say that I'm still eyed with suspicion for being different.

GRAEME LE SAUX, Blackburn defender, shortly before his on-pitch fisticuffs with team-mate David Batty over a remark the latter made, 1995.

I decided it was time to stop when I began feeling exhausted after games. The other lads have something to eat and a game of cards. I find a quiet corner on the coach and fall asleep.

ALVIN MARTIN, West Ham defender, on deciding to retire, 1995.

I still watch the first-team games and always give the lads encouragement, but you have mixed emotions. You want them to win, but how are you going to get back in if they keep doing well?

JASON DOZZELL, Tottenham midfielder, on life as a reserve, 1995.

I hate losing and I don't tend to speak much after a defeat. Footballers must be murder to live with – everyone I know is grumpy.

CHRIS SUTTON, Blackburn striker, 1994.

I just wish all this (the footballer's life) could last a bit longer, that's all. Playing till you're 45, that'd suit me.

DARREN ANDERTON, Tottenham and England midfielder, 1995.

CHAPTER 5

Philosophers Utd

When the seagulls follow the trawler it is because they think sardines will be thrown into the sea.

ERIC CANTONA addressing the media,
after escaping jail sentence, 1995.

If a Frenchman goes on about seagulls, trawlers and sardines, he's called a philosopher. I'd just be called a short Scottish bum talking crap.

GORDON STRACHAN, Leeds midfielder and former
team-mate of Cantona's, 1995.

Cantona is always chasing Rimbauds. (With apologies to Dorothy Parker).

One man's *metier* is another man's *poisson*.

READERS' responses in The Independent to Cantona's 'seagulls,
trawlers and sardines' remark, 1995.

If somebody in the crowd spits at you, you've just got to swallow it.

GARY LINEKER, quoting the advice of his former Leicester manager,
Gordon Milne, 1995.

I like to take time off to stop and smell the flowers. That's my way.

IVAN GOLAC, Dundee United manager,
after reaching Scottish Cup final, 1994.

My career has been like the migrating woodcock really. You never know what's in front of you. You've got all the shooters and the storms trying to whack you down, but in the end you just want to get to new fields.

VINNIE JONES, Wimbledon midfielder, 1995.

Q: One wish?
A: Apart from world peace, a long injury-free career.

GARETH SOUTHGATE, Aston Villa defender,
in programme questionnaire, 1995.

You've got to take the rough with the smooth. It's like love and hate, war and peace, all that bollocks.

IAN WRIGHT, Arsenal striker, on being restored to the England team against Romania, 1995.

What it does, Brian, is make an impossible job harder.

RON ATKINSON, Coventry manager, 1995.

Football is a fertility festival. Eleven sperm trying to get into the egg. I feel sorry for the goalkeeper.

BJORK, Icelandic pop singer, 1995.

If we win, it'll be a nationwide orgasm.

JESUS GIL, Atletico Madrid president, before derby with Real, 1995.

There's a lot of shouting in the QPR dressing room before a match, but I just try to relax. I go into the toilets and read the whole programme.

TREVOR SINCLAIR, QPR midfielder, 1995.

That was a cross. If he meant it as a shot I'll drop my trousers in Burton's window.

MICK McCARTHY, Millwall manager, on goal by Swindon's Jan Fjortoft, 1995.

Of course I meant it to go in. If the Millwall manager likes, I'll come with him to the shop – it should make a good picture.

JAN FJORTOFT, Swindon striker, 1995.

FOOTBALL MATCHES ARE LIKE DAYS OF THE WEEK. IT CAN'T BE SUNDAY
EVERY DAY. THERE ARE ALSO MONDAYS AND TUESDAYS.

GEORGE WEAH, Milan forward, 1995.

The good people of Suffolk will be looking forward to this.

BOBBY GOULD, Radio 5 Live summariser,
before Norwich v Bayern Munich, 1993.

Last year I had a foot operation. Then in my first game my thigh went in the warm up. This season I'm going to play it by ear.

JOHN ALDRIDGE, Tranmere and Republic of Ireland striker, 1995.

We've heard that Keith Curle will be out for six weeks because of an ankle injury, but that's the sort of blow you've got to take on the chin.

ALAN BALL, Manchester City manager, 1995.

If they keep ramming it down his throat then the ball's in his court.

ROY EVANS, Liverpool manager, on the efforts of Stan Collymore
and Robbie Fowler to impress England manager Terry Venables, 1996.

I just wonder what would have happened if the shirt had been on the other foot.

MIKE WALKER, Norwich manager, complaining that refereeing
decisions went against his side in defeat by Manchester United, 1994.

No one hands you cups on a plate.

TERRY McDERMOTT, Newcastle manager, 1995.

That chance came him to him on a plate out of the blue.

GLENN HODDLE, Sky TV summariser, England v Nigeria, 1994.

Shelbourne are obviously having serious trouble with Bohemians' five-man back four.

EAMONN GREGG, Irish TV analyst, 1995.

Great striking partnerships come in pairs.

NIGEL SPACKMAN, Chelsea midfielder working as TV pundit, 1994.

If I played for Scotland my grandma would be the proudest woman in the country – if she wasn't dead.

MARK CROSSLEY, Barnsley-born Nottingham Forest goalkeeper,
on his eligibility for the Scots, 1995.

What I said to them at half-time would be unprintable on radio.

GERRY FRANCIS, Tottenham manager, to Radio 5 Live after his team
came from behind to beat West Ham, 1995.

And that's a priceless goal worth millions of pounds.

ALAN PARRY, ITV commentator, on the European Cup final, 1995.

In Cup competitions, Jack will always have a chance of beating Goliath.

TERRY BUTCHER, Sunderland manager, in his programme column, 1993.

People are going to think that not only are centre-halves useless and ugly, but we're also thick.

COLIN HENDRY, Blackburn centre-back, on losing at Trivial Pursuit game
set up by Goal magazine, 1996.

This is the only club in the country I would have signed for.

ANDY COLE, on joining Manchester United from Newcastle, January, 1995.

This is the only club in the country I would have signed for.

KEITH GILLESPIE, on joining Newcastle from Manchester United, January, 1995.

They're going through my drawers line by line.

GRAHAM KELLY, FA chief executive, on the raid by
trading standards officers of his Lancaster Gate HQ, 1996.

I'm only 33 but my hair is 83.

ANDY RITCHIE, balding Oldham striker, 1994

I tell my players that they've made a happy man very old.

JIMMY NICHOLL, Raith Rovers manager, 1995.

The game's never over till the fat striker scores.

JOHN ROBERTSON, Hearts striker,
on his last-minute equaliser at Hibernian, 1995.

It's not the end of the World – just the end of Europe.

ROY EVANS, Liverpool manager on defeat by Brondby in the UEFA Cup, 1995.

I consider this defeat to be the mother of future victories.

> ANTONIO OLIVEIRA, Portugal manager, after 1-0 defeat
> by the Republic of Ireland, 1995.

The road to ruin is paved with excuses.

> BOBBY GOULD, Coventry manager, after defeat by Leeds, 1993.

They're better than us because their players have been fed on bananas since birth whereas we had to wait until after the revolution to eat them.

> ANTON DOBOS, Steaua Bucharest player, after
> Champions League defeat by Juventus, 1995.

How do I feel? Lower than a snake's belly, that's how I feel.

> STEVE McMAHON, Swindon player-manager, on his side's relegation, 1995.

We were starting to bleed. We were like a boxer having a bad time. They might not knock us out, but the referee might stop the fight on cuts.

> KEVIN KEEGAN, Newcastle manager, on his side's dismal
> first half at Aston Villa, 1995.

We didn't play well, but sometimes you have to take the crumbs off the table.

> KEEGAN after Newcastle's win at Coventry, 1996.

It was a case of the circus coming to town, but the lions and tigers didn't turn up.

> KEEGAN after Newcastle's submission to Manchester United, 1995.

I felt like the garrison commander at Rorke's Drift when the Zulus came pouring over the hill.

> ALAN BALL, Manchester City manager, on his first training session
> with a squad of 42 players, 1995.

Going behind that early made it like trying to run uphill in treacle.

> HOWARD WILKINSON, Leeds manager, after FA Cup defeat at Old Trafford, 1995.

Alex Totten (Kilmarnock manager) sent me to Coventry for so long I thought I'd signed for them.

> ANDY MILLEN, Hibernian defender, after leaving the Ayrshire club, 1995.

I didn't want to play another 300 games in the Premiership with mediocre players and be up against it. I wanted the ball to be up the opposing end so that I could get my cigars out at the back.

TONY ADAMS, Arsenal captain, on the importance of bringing in Platt and Bergkamp, 1995.

When the Captain said there was a problem at the back I thought he meant me and Steve Bould.

TONY ADAMS on a delayed flight back from Copenhagen, 1994.

Q: Does it suit you to be the underdogs.
A: I must tell you I do not like for me or my players to be called dogs.

BORA MILUTINOVIC, United States' Serbian coach, at press conference during World Cup finals, 1994.

I don't even know where Portsmouth is. All I know is a lot of sailors live there.

FRANK MALONEY, boxing promoter, denying reported takeover bid, 1995.

Being at Mansfield is a bit like being in pantomime, only with fewer people watching.

DALEY THOMPSON, former Olympic decathlon champion, on playing for Mansfield reserves at 38, 1995.

They reckon we caught Spurs at a good time because they haven't been doing too well. But look at us – we haven't won since Hitler invaded Poland.

CHRIS TURNER, Peterborough manager, after draw with Spurs, 1994.

Dani's so good looking that when he came on, Villa didn't know whether to mark him or bonk him.

HARRY REDKNAPP, West Ham manager, on his Portuguese signing, 1996.

We were forced to play so many youngsters that you had to burp and wind them after each game.

MICK McCARTHY, Millwall manager, 1995.

I like the warmth of the town. Why are people surprised that I like Grimsby? I like everybody in the place and the fans do not jump on my back all the time.

IVANO BONETTI, Grimsby's former Juventus midfielder, 1995.

I've been playing 15 years and it's only today I realised that I'm left-footed.

DAVE WATSON, Everton defender, after his 25-yard left-footed shot
earned a point at Arsenal, 1995.

I thought they had slipped Steve McQueen on.

DAVE BASSETT, Sheffield United manager, after two Wolves goals in a minute, 1995.

It's been like having a big car and then not having the money to buy any petrol.

BOBBY CLARK, New Zealand's Scottish manager, on the
financial constraints that forced his resignation, 1995.

I drive a Corvette, not a Volkswagen or an Audi in Germany. This must be because of my American blood. I watch the Superbowl and get goose bumps and water in my eyes whenever I hear Whitney Houston. This makes me American, yes?

THOMAS DOOLEY, German-born US midfielder, on why he was happy
to represent his adopted country, 1994.

My love affair with football, which started when I was a two or three-year-old, will hopefully continue until the day I die. But you can sometimes have a love affair and live apart, can't you?

GRAHAM TAYLOR, in between England and Wolves jobs, 1994.

I looked up at the clock and it was five to 11. I thought to myself: 'I shouldn't be playing football at five to 11.'

COLIN COOPER, Nottingham Forest defender, after extra time at Lyon, 1995.

What do I think of Brighton? I think the beach is all right.

JEFF KING, Canvey Island manager, after drawing with
Second Division Brighton in the FA Cup, 1995.

Q: Who would you least want to invite to a party?
A: Any Labour politician.

TONY COTTEE, West Ham striker, in programme questionnaire, 1995.

I thought the Mafia only existed in Italy.

DIEGO MARADONA after being tested for drugs in Spain, 1993.

God is a Bulgarian.

> HRISTO STOICHKOV after his country's win on penalties
> against Mexico in the World Cup, 1994.

God is still a Bulgarian, but the referee was French.

> STOICHKOV after Bulgaria were denied claims
> for a second penalty during defeat by Italy.

He'll be the most famous Greek for years, even though he's Argentinian.

> RON ATKINSON, ITV pundit, after Panathinaikos,
> managed by Juan Rocha, won at Ajax 1996

Not only do the South Koreans' names sound the same but they all look similar, don't they?

> ALAN PARRY, ITV commentator, World Cup finals, 1994.

You know what I was dreading in the World Cup? That the final should be between Germany and Saudi Arabia. I mean, which side should a good Jew support?

> IVOR DEMBINA, comedian, Edinburgh Festival, 1994.

The air conditioning was good.

> RUNE HAUGE, Norwegian agent, after giving evidence to the
> FA's hearing into the George Graham affair, 1995.

Let us not forget that the place of truth for an athlete is, and always will be, the stadium.

> ERIC CANTONA, from La Philosophie de Cantona, 1995.

Football as popular culture is a space of intertextuality.

> RICHARD HAYNES, author, The Football Imagination:
> The Rise of Fanzine Culture, 1996

Most players would give their right arm for his left foot.

> MARK LAWRENSON, Radio 5 Live summariser,
> discussing Blackburn's Jason Wilcox, 1996.

We all know that in football, you stand still if you go backwards.

> PETER REID, Sunderland manager, 1996.

CHAPTER 6

The Middle Men

Referees

I played full-back in rugby union, wicketkeeper in cricket and goal-keeper in football, the positions in which you stand out. On reflection, refereeing is a bit like that. We're very much loners.

PHILIP DON, Middlesex referee, 1995.

My wife, who was in the stand, told me that at one stage the entire row in front of her stood up and gave me the V-sign. I asked her what she did and she said she didn't want them to know who she was so she stood up and joined in.

NEIL MIDGLEY, retired referee, recalling his First Division 'debut',
in Derick Allsop, The Game of Their Lives, 1995.

Most jobs get easier the longer you do them, as you get more experienced. I've been a local government officer for more than 20 years and it gets easier. This is getting harder. The pressure has increased, the pace of the game is greater. There is so much money involved, so much at stake.

STEPHEN LODGE, Barnsley referee, 1995.

Why should I allow a referee to do things which destroy my life? When managers make mistakes, they get sacked. What happens to referees? He is probably going home in his car now thinking about where he's going to referee next week.

JOE KINNEAR, Wimbledon manager, bemoaning the performance
of Harrow official David Elleray, 1995.

The referee has got me the sack. Thank him for that.

> GRAHAM TAYLOR, then England manager, to linesman and Fifa official
> at World Cup qualifying defeat by the Netherlands, in Channel 4's
> *Cutting Edge* documentary, 1994.

Only one person in the ground thought it was a penalty and he was the wrong one.

> JOE ROYLE, Everton manager, after a spot-kick award to Millwall
> had turned a Coca-Cola Cup tie, 1995.

The first lad deserved a yellow card and as for the second, well, I've seen it on the box and it's a bloody joke. We'll end up with four players on each side. It's all about contact, for Christ's sake.

> ALAN BIRCHENALL, Leicester City commercial manager, taking to the Tannoy
> at half-time in match v Coventry after referee Keith Cooper dismissed
> a player from either side, 1994.

In all fairness, the referee had a complete cerebral failure.

> RICK HOLDEN, Oldham winger, after defeat at Southend, 1995.

The official today was a muppet.

> IAN WRIGHT, Arsenal striker, on a referee who booked him at Norwich, 1994.

If this had happened in a South American country, he'd have been shot at half-time.

> MEL MACHIN, Bournemouth manager, on Orpington referee
> Barry Knight after he sent off two of his team, 1995.

A film called *Passport To Terror* will follow and I think this referee will be in it.

> DESMOND LYNAM, BBC-TV presenter on a card-happy display by
> Syria's Jamal Al-Sharif in Bulgaria v Mexico match, World Cup finals, 1994.

My certain feeling is of being raped week in, week out by referees and linesmen, and it just cannot go on.

> SAM HAMMAM, Wimbledon owner, claiming victimisation, 1995.

I have to hand it to Manchester United. They have the best players — and the best referees.

> HAMMAM, 1995.

Referees take from the small clubs and give to the big boys. The facts of life are that the dice is loaded against the poorer people. It is a fact that clubs like Manchester United and Newcastle get more points every season than they have earned.

HAMMAM, 1995.

Our conclusion is that there are referees for the big countries and not for the small ones.

ROGER VAN DEN STOCK, Belgian FA official, after Belgium were refused
a 'blatant' penalty v Germany, World Cup finals, 1994.

I've seen referees who aren't fit to officiate on Copacabana beach.

GERSON, former Brazilian player, at World Cup finals, 1994.

Referees are part of the game and the perfect referee doesn't exist. They're entitled to have a bad day... It's one man against 90,000 people and 22 actors, and a percentage of calls (decisions) will always be wrong.

GUIDO TOGNONI, Fifa spokesman, defending standards
at the World Cup finals, 1994.

I complain about referees as long and loud as anyone, but I wouldn't want their job for a gold pig.

MICK McCARTHY, Millwall manager, 1995.

Fuck off! Are you blind ref?

CHORUS of players and fans in *Playing Away*, Opera North production, 1994.

I do swear a lot, but the advantage is that having played abroad, I can choose a different language from the referee's.

JURGEN KLINSMANN, Tottenham and Germany striker, 1995.

When a player says 'shit' as he trips over the ball, it does not usually mean that he has slipped on a dog poop.

BISHOP OF HASLINGDEN, former referee, in *The Football Referee* magazine, 1995.

I'm having a crap game and nothing you say will alter it.

IAN BORRETT, Norfolk referee, to Crystal Palace manager
Alan Smith during match, 1993.

I used to think that getting a televised game was a real bonus. Now, like most referees, I would rather avoid them like the plague.

STEPHEN LODGE, Barnsley referee, on 'trial by action replay', 1995.

I've seen harder tackles in the half-time pie queue than the ones punished in games.

GEORGE FULSTON, Falkirk chairman, on his side's poor disciplinary record, 1995.

The day I had to book Gazza for celebrating scoring a goal was the last straw. We're being programmed like robots with a list of instructions.

JIM McGILVRAY, Scottish League referee, announcing his decision to resign, 1996.

If the Scottish FA is accused of creating robots by issuing instructions, then we plead guilty. The set of instructions is called the laws of the game.

JIM FARRY, SFA chief executive, responding to McGilvray.

Some of the decisions we have been getting lately are so bizarre they are bordering on the *Twilight Zone*.

SAM HAMMAM, Wimbledon owner, calling for an inquiry into the refereeing of his club's games, 1995.

I do like Selhurst Park. There's a Sainsbury's right next to the ground so it's an ideal chance to get some of the weekend shopping out of the way.

DAVID ELLERAY, Middlesex referee, 1996.

It's a sorry state when the referee feels he's got equal billing with Eric Cantona. Eric came through his test, I'm not sure the referee did.

ROY EVANS, Liverpool manager, after Cantona's return from his eight-month ban against Liverpool, 1995. Referee David Elleray said before the game that he would be the focus of attention alongside Cantona.

Look at it this way, son. What would you say if you got run through the chest when your mind was only on taking a corner kick.

TERRY PATTISON, Chiswick District League referee, abandoning the match after substituted player returned wielding a sword, 1995.

Match abandoned in 60th minute due to intervention of knife maniac.

PATTISON's report to the league.

I'm very concerned that hostile swordplay would have a bad effect in the middle of the match.

PATTISON explaining his decision to a spectator, 1995.

To get the linesman, who was deaf, to listen to me, I merely threw a little water on him.

DIEGO MARADONA after being sent off in Argentinian League match, 1995.

I saw someone eyeing me in the pub. I asked: 'Do I know you?' He said: 'You should. You sent me off today'.

SONYA HOME, referee, 1995.

Agents

When people ask my wife what I do she tells them I'm a Kwik-Fit fitter rather than admit I'm an agent.

JON HOLMES, agent, 1996.

Dogs, worms, vermin.

JOE KINNEAR, Wimbledon manager, on agents, 1995.

(Manchester) United were bad payers in the Seventies. They had the mentality that footballers would play for them for nothing. People moan about agents but I wish they'd been around in my day.

STUART PEARSON, former United and England striker, 1995.

Eric Hall is the one behind all the problems we've had, with his snide little whispers to this player and that player, saying they should get away. All that weasel sees is pound signs.

VINNIE JONES, Wimbledon captain, blaming the agent for his
club's problems, 1995. Jones later apologised to Hall.

Eric (Hall) doesn't exactly present himself as Mister bleedin' sensible, does he? He's a good laugh, but he don't look like the most trustworthy individual. He's all right. The players like him, and if someone's dopey enough to have Eric as his agent, good luck to him.

DAVE BASSETT, Sheffield United manager, 1995.

I once had a player's agent meet me at Palace hoping to improve what I thought was already a healthy contract. These are the exact words he said to me: 'Well you have to understand that if my boy doesn't get what he wants then he will be an unhappy player, and we all know how an unhappy player plays'.

STEVE COPPELL, former Crystal Palace manager, 1993.

There's always a tendency for players to underprice themselves. No one likes to go in and say 'I'm worth this or that'. Neither do you want to be at loggerheads with a club you're working for, so it's better if someone else does the talking for you and leaves you to do the playing.

RAY WILKINS, Queen's Park Rangers midfielder, 1993.

Q: WHO'S YOUR FAVOURITE PLAYER?
A: I DON'T KNOW ANYTHING ABOUT FOOTBALL.
I CAN'T SAY.

ERIC HALL, 'monster' agent, in interview with
Total Football magazine, 1995.

We come out of school early, at 15, not the most educated people. In our early twenties we're earning money that professional people are striving to earn in their forties. For all the good advice your dad can give, he doesn't know the ins and outs of contracts.

DAVID O'LEARY, Arsenal defender, 1993.

When I was in showbiz and record promoting, everyone was openly paid for their efforts and no one considered it sleazy. Agents were welcomed as a vital part of the system. It's only because the football authorities refused to accept it that the problems started.

ERIC HALL, agent, 1995.

Players tell me they can never get hold of Gordon Taylor (players' union chief executive) because he's always in meetings. I'm available 365 days a year, including Christmas Day. Only me and Father Christmas actually work and he finishes early anyway.

HALL, 1993.

I now believe in Father Christmas, I really do. I owe him (Jean-Marc Bosman) a monster Christmas present.

HALL, after the European Union's highest court ruled that the game's transfer system was illegal, 1995.

CHAPTER 7

Supporting Cast

Every thousandth person created, God unhinges their heads, scoops out their brains and then issues them to a football club (as supporters).

MIKE BATESON, Torquay chairman, 1996.

Football's getting too polished and nice and trendy now. You get media people in London who say, 'Football is the new rock 'n' roll'. For all us working class, it's a way of life, always has been.

SEAN BEAN, actor and Sheffield United fan, 1996.

Fans are interested in their team being successful. If they wanted to see entertaining football rather than get results week in, week out, why don't all the Arsenal fans support Spurs or Chelsea.

DAVE BASSETT, Sheffield United manager, 1995.

I'm in charge, not you. If it doesn't work out I know what the bottom line is. If you want to be manager of Newcastle, apply for the job.

KEVIN KEEGAN, Newcastle manager, to fans angry over the transfer of Andy Cole, 1995.

I began my career with Polesworth Swifts and seven years later I remain loyal to the club. My honours include most improved player 1991 and supporters' player 1992. Do not make the mistake of letting me slip through your fingers as Brian Clough did. Do you want another decade of international ridicule?

PAUL ROWLING, 14-year-old Tamworth schoolboy, in letter to the FA
applying for England manager's job, 1996.

I thought I'd seen it all when it comes to the fickleness of football folk. Then I heard the Spurs fans singing: 'There's only one Alan Sugar'.

MICK McCARTHY, Millwall manager, 1994.

As a Celtic fan I've spent a quite inordinate and rationally unjustifiable amount of time just thinking about football – daydreaming and intellectualising – with even more synaptic brain-cell connections being devoted to the sport than to sex, although they do occasionally overlap (and I don't just mean when reciting obscure team formations from 1982 in my head to postpone premature ejaculation).

DAVID BENNIE, author, *Not Playing for Celtic*, 1995.

When we won the League in 89 it was the most cosmic thing that had ever happened. Better than any orgasm ever.

EMMA YOUNG, Arsenal fan, in Tom Watt,
The End: 80 years of Life on Arsenal's North Bank, 1993.

I got some girl's pants through the post the other day but I didn't like them...well, they didn't fit to be honest.

JAMIE REDKNAPP, Liverpool midfielder, on his fan mail, 1995.

Football is the only subject that can induce a bloke to swank about his fidelity.

HARRY PEARSON, author and Middlesbrough fan, in
The Far Corner: A Mazy Dribble Through North-east Football, 1994.

Visiting a prostitute is in the same league as fishing or football as a leisure activity.

HILARY KINNELL, Birmingham Research Project, 1993.

I love Newcastle, I love that raw passion. I remember being in Newcastle once and hearing newspaper vendors shouting: 'Sensation! Cole Toe Injury'. Sensation? Most vendors use the word for 'Major Resigns' or 'Aids Spreading over Country'. It's unbelievable. Glasgow's like that.

ALEX FERGUSON, Manchester United manager, 1995.

The Glaswegian definition of an atheist: a bloke who goes to a Rangers-Celtic match to watch the football.

SANDY STRANG, Rangers supporter, in Stephen Walsh, *Voices of the Old Firm*, 1995.

For a while I did unite Rangers and Celtic fans. There were people in both camps who hated me.

> MAURICE JOHNSTON, Hearts striker, on his spells on both sides of
> Glasgow's sectarian divide, 1994.

Ibrox is a tough place to perform in. We have players who actually prefer playing away because of the nature of the Rangers support. I prefer our away following – they get behind the team far better.

> RICHARD GOUGH, Rangers captain, 1995.

I'm not a violent man but as soon as you see the first flash of green or a Republic (of Ireland) jersey, something inside of you snaps.

> RANGERS SUPPORTER, interviewed on Channel 4 documentary
> Football, Faith and Flutes, 1995.

They call themselves Protestants. But they just say that because they want to be different from Catholics. Most of them are atheists.

> CELTIC SUPPORTER,Football, Faith and Flutes, 1995.

I love the people on Merseyside, even the Liverpool fans. After all, I'm a Liverpool fan myself when they're not playing Everton.

> DANIEL AMOKACHI, Everton's Nigerian striker, 1995.

When we went away there were all the supporters' coaches from places like Dover and Falmouth. I'd never even heard of Falmouth. It seeps into you. I like that passion.

> ALEX FERGUSON, United manager, 1995.

Traffic jam on the M5 – Man United must be at home.

> MANCHESTER CITY FANS' joke about United's alleged lack of Mancunian support, 1995.

Inverness is such a terrible place you have to do something on a Saturday afternoon.

> DAVID McDONALD, Inverness Caledonian fanzine editor, admitting he would watch
> Caledonian Thistle, even though he campaigned against Caley's merger with Thistle, 1994.

Q: What is the craziest request you have ever had from a fan?
A: Can you do your brother's autograph.

> CARL HODDLE, Barnet midfielder and brother of Glenn, in Sun questionnaire, 1995.

As much as I love women and music, my first love will always be football.

> ROD STEWART, pop singer, failed Brentford trialist and Scotland fan, 1995.

Q: What was the first gig you went to?
A: Wolves v Moscow Dynamo, 9 November 1955 (Wolves won 2-1).

> ROBERT PLANT, former vocalist with the rock group Led Zeppelin,
> in interview with *Q* magazine, 1993.

I did my grieving when I was kicked out. Frankly I'm more concerned about how Port Vale do in the FA Cup tonight.

> ROBBIE WILLIAMS, former member of Take That, on the group's break-up, 1996.
> Vale beat Everton, the Cup holders.

After Sky started covering live matches that ruled out doing concerts on Saturday, Sunday, Monday and Wednesday, and meant my agent has got Tuesday, Thursday and Friday to book me into places – as long as I can get back here (Villa Park).

> NIGEL KENNEDY, classical violinist and Aston Villa fanatic, 1995.

It says on my birth certificate that I was born in the borough of West Bromwich, in the district of West Bromwich. I said all right, all right, I'll support the bloody Albion – there's no need to twist my arm.

> FRANK SKINNER, comedian, 1995.

During the kerfuffle over Michael Heseltine's pit closures, Brian (Clough) led a march past my surgery, which is a short walk from Forest's ground. At the time, Forest were heading for relegation and I threatened to lead a counter march past the ground.

> KENNETH CLARKE MP, Nottingham Forest fan, in *Football and the Commons People*, 1995.

Famous Carlisle United Fans: Melvyn Bragg (unless he's in London, then he's an Arsenal fan) and Hunter Davies (unless he's in London, then he's a Spurs fan).

> *TOTAL FOOTBALL* magazine, 1995.

I've got this tattoo on my left arm that says '100 per cent Blade'. When we were filming the steamy scenes in *Lady Chatterley's Lover*, Ken Russell used to hide it with a strategically placed fern.

> SEAN BEAN, actor and Sheffield United fan, 1996.

I was in the Leeds end, chanting and going mad, and the fans were saying: 'Hang on – what's he doing here?'

> NOEL WHELAN, Coventry striker, on continuing to support his previous club, 1996.

We had to let the fans in. None of us knew how to play the fiddle.

> PAUL McGRATH, Republic of Ireland defender, recalling how Irish supporters partied with the team until the early hours after 1988 win v England, 1995.

And all the runs that Kinky makes are winding
And all the goals that Uwe scores are blinding
Cos maybe
You're gonna be the one that saves me
And after all
You're my Alan Ball.

> MANCHESTER CITY FANS' SONG, to the tune of Oasis' 'Wonderwall', 1996.
> 'Kinky' is Georgiou Kinkladze.

Piss in your water, we're gonna piss in your water...

> NEWCASTLE FANS' SONG to Leeds supporters at time of operation to transport water from the North-east to drought-stricken Yorkshire, 1995.

If it wasn't for the English, you'd be Krauts.

> NOTTINGHAM FOREST FANS' SONG at Lyon, France, 1995.

We all agree, Fettis is better than Shearer.

> HULL FANS' SONG after their goalkeeper, Alan Fettis, scored twice as a striker when he had a broken thumb, 1995.

Where were you when you were shit?

> RIVAL FANS' SONG to Blackburn fans, 1995.

Palace, Palace, Who the F*** are Palace?

> CHARLTON FANS' SONG, to the tune of 'Living Next Door to Alice', 1996.

Can we play you every week?

> BOLTON FANS' SONG at Middlesbrough as their team won 4-1 to end a long losing run, 1996.

Jesus is a Wiganner

> WIGAN ATHLETIC FANS' BANNER after the club signed Jesus Seba from Zaragoza, 1995.

Stop the Nuclear tests at Muroroa – Do them in Naples

PADOVA FANS' BANNER, 1995.

BURNLEY – TWINNED WITH TRELLEBORGS

TOWN SIGN amended by Burnley fans after the Swedish part-timers
of Trelleborgs beat Blackburn, 1994.

We want one! We want one!

IPSWICH FANS' CHANT at Old Trafford in response to Manchester United
supporters' call of 'We want 10!' when their side led 9-0, 1995.

Birch! You couldn't cross a pools coupon!

SPECTATOR at Wolves, 1994.

Trying to explain why we hate Palace is like trying to explain why
grass is green and vomit lumpy. We just do.

ATTILA THE STOCKBROKER, poet and Brighton supporter, 1995.

A crop-headed youth of such vast proportions that any Norwegians
present must have been tempted to harpoon him and take him home
for supper came into the Gallowgate eating a pie. It was one of those
special football pies with asbestos-grey pastry that cracks to release
the odour of a 1,000-year-old tomb.

HARRY PEARSON, author, *The Far Corner: A Mazy Dribble Through North-East Football*, 1994.

Last year we test-marketed scampi at Blackburn, but you could count
the number we sold on one hand.

PAUL CROWTON, managing director of football's largest stadium caterers, Lindleys, 1994.

Football violence is like smoking. If you try it once and hate it, you
don't do it again, but if you try it once and like it, it's bloody hard to
give up.

DOUGIE & EDDY BRIMSON, authors, on their life as
Watford hooligans, *Everywhere We Go*, 1996.

He told me I was a dead man and that I wouldn't get out of The Den
alive. Then he said I was fat. I said: 'Have you looked at yourself lately?'

KEVIN PRESSMAN, Sheffield Wednesday goalkeeper,
threatened by a pitch-invader at Millwall, 1995.

If Cantona had jumped into our crowd he'd never have come out alive.

ALEX RAE, Millwall midfielder, 1995.

After Birmingham's first goal, one of their fans came out and hit one of our subs in the face. You can imagine what might have happened if that had happened at our place.

MICK McCARTHY, Millwall manager, after match marred
by crowd disturbances at St Andrew's, 1995.

I must have done all right for them to gob all over me.

STEVE JONES, Bournemouth striker, after running a gauntlet
of Birmingham fans, 1994.

The thought zapped me even as I went down: 'That's it, your career's finished'. The stretcher took forever to arrive. The trip to the brand new – who cares – medical suite even longer. As I was being carried along the touchline, a Bristol City fan leaned out from the crowd: 'That's your career over, you bastard,' he crowed. 'You'll never play again'.

GARRY NELSON, Charlton striker, in Left Foot Forward:
A Year in the Life of a Journeyman Footballer, 1995.

At the FA Cup final I went over to take a kick where the Chelsea fans were and they started chucking things at me. Nothing unusual there, except these weren't the usual plastic cups and cans, they were sticks of celery and sweetcorn. I don't know what that was about, but it made me laugh to think of them popping into greengrocers' shops on the way to Wembley.

RYAN GIGGS, Manchester United winger, 1994.

At Anfield, they throw 50p pieces at me, yelling abuse. I have my own way of dealing with that: I put the ball down, take one step, kick it and then run for the safety of the penalty area, where I've only got Neil Ruddock to worry about.

GIGGS on Liverpool fans, 1994.

MERCI POUR CANTONA, SCUM

MANCHESTER UNITED FANS' BANNER at Leeds, 1994.

Do they hate us? You go to take a corner at Elland Road and you've got 15,000 horrible skinheads in their end yelling murder at you.

GIGGS on Leeds fans, 1994.

I am 100 per cent sure our fans won't abuse Cantona. For a start, Manchester United haven't given us any tickets for the match.

JOHN BARNES, Liverpool midfielder, deflecting fears about Cantona's reception on his return from his eight-month ban, 1995.

The English stick their psychos in Broadmoor, while the Welsh put theirs in Ninian Park.

THERE'S ONLY ONE F IN FULHAM fanzine, awarding Cardiff City fans 0 out of 10 in their Best Fans poll, 1995.

It was disgraceful. Every one of our team stopped. It was such a bad decision you can't call it a decision. It used to be difficult to get a throw-in at Anfield, and it's becoming the same here.

FRANCIS LEE, chairman, Manchester City, on the Newcastle crowd's alleged part in a goal during an FA Cup tie, 1995.

The atmosphere in the USA isn't right. The American public look at a game as a day out to eat hot-dogs and popcorn. In Europe the fans can't eat because their stomachs are tight with tension.

ANTONIO MATERRESE, Italian FA president, at the World Cup finals in the United States, 1994.

There were three countries in the world that would have caused us logistical and security problems, so we're very pleased they won't be coming: Iran, Iraq and England.

ALAN ROTHENBERG, chairman, United States World Cup committee, 1994.

People are faking injuries, coming through the gates on crutches, then pulling their banners from their underwear and flying them from a crutch. We can't do a thing. You can't take someone's crutches away from them. They might be genuinely injured or disabled.

NEW JERSEY STATE POLICE SPOKESMAN on the ingenuity of fans without tickets during the World Cup finals, 1994.

Keep the television down low. When you see a great goal, keep your emotions under control. Don't shout loudly or applaud. You must especially guard against accidents happening because of lack of sleep.

EDITORIAL in *People's Daily of China*, during World Cup finals, 1994.

It (the World Cup finals) was a throwback to the Fifties to see how much 'rival' spectators enjoyed mixing with each other. The only trouble I saw was at a concert in the Dodgers Stadium.

RON ATKINSON, ITV pundit and Aston Villa manager, in the United States, 1994.

I think more people would have been killed if we hadn't gone all-seater. We had a disaster about every 15 years and that's not a price worth paying. I'd rather sit than die!

NICK HORNBY, writer, in Tom Watt, *The End: 80 Years of Life on Arsenal's North Bank*, 1993.

In 10 years' time they'll be sitting in the stand, watching the match, and their children will say: 'Daddy, did you really stand over there, in the wind and rain? And did the man behind you urinate in your back pocket? And did you have a pie from that awful shop and a pint of beer thrust in your hand on a cold day?' The kids just will not understand.

SIR JOHN HALL, Newcastle chairman, 1995.

Once I saw a Thistle fan spend the whole game with his nose in Dostoyevsky. It was *Crime and Punishment* – clearly this chap was a season-ticket holder.

MORVEN GOW, Partick Thistle supporter, in Bell's whisky advert, 1996.

CHAPTER 8

Women With Balls

The Future is Feminine.

SEPP BLATTER, Fifa general secretary, after the Women's World Cup, 1995.

I am probably more male than most men. I was brought up going to watch boxing and football.

KARREN BRADY, Birmingham City managing director, 1995.

Men say things like: 'Oh, it's just a bunch of dykes'...I hate the fact that there are girls who'd love to play but don't because the image is so bad.

JULIE FOUDY, United States captain, 1995.

I did ask one company for a pair of boots for the World Cup, but I got turned down. It's funny when you think that some footballers get paid millions for endorsing footwear.

CLARE TAYLOR, England midfielder, before the Women's World Cup finals, 1995.

I would very quickly swap places with Gascoigne and Shearer if it meant getting their money. But I said no to Inter Milan when I had the chance to join their women's team.

CLARE TAYLOR

I want to win a little too badly. I've had concussion, I've had teeth knocked out and I've needed eight operations on my knees. It was only after the sixth that I realised I didn't have to win every single tackle. It's not easy to accept that are situations on the field where the risks aren't worth taking.

MICHELLE AKERS-STAHL, United States women's team captain, 1995.

I don't know if I enjoy being in the limelight, but being England centre-forward, it's inevitable. I get recognised in the street – and not just where I live.

KAREN WALKER, Doncaster Belles and England striker, 1993.

There's still that blinkered view that all women footballers have thighs like joints of ham and make rugby players look like flake adverts.

MARIANNE SPACEY, Arsenal and England striker, 1995

It's left us with a massive hole to fill.

VIC AKERS, Arsenal coach, on the news that Spacey was pregnant, 1995.

Trollops on tour.

SIGN in bus carrying Manchester United women's team, 1996.

You come across different sorts of referees in women's football. Some are avuncular, enthusiastic and fair; some use the game to prove they can control women.

ALYSON RUDD, Leyton Orient Ladies striker and *Times* writer, 1994.

For our game the referee was pleasant enough, but a little erratic, a bit nonplussed by 22 fiercely competitive women.

ALYSON RUDD

It's harder to get them psyched up for a match. Men are more arrogant and more confident. The girls question their ability more.

TED COPELAND, England women's coach, 1995.

After all, this is not a game for little ladies.

PLACIDO DOMINGO, opera singer and football fan, defending rugged Spanish tackling during World Cup finals, 1994.

Talking of football being a man's game, we welcome, on her League debut, lineswoman Wendy Toms. I question the wisdom of a woman official for the single fact of the problems which some clubs will have in arranging changing facilities...I look forward to the day when the entire line-up of officials for a given match is all-female.

MIKE BATESON, Torquay chairman, programme column, 1994.

My role consists of playing mother while remaining an iron woman. That's not easy.

KARREN BRADY, managing director, Birmingham City,
in interview with *Elle* magazine, 1995.

If it wasn't for Tracy, I'd be an 18-stone alcoholic bricklayer playing for Penicuik Athletic.

ANDY GORAM, Rangers and Scotland goalkeeper,
paying tribute to his second wife, 1995.

I'll probably get home and find that the wife has left me.

LEE BUTLER, substitute Barnsley goalkeeper, after letting in five goals
in 38 minutes against Birmingham, 1995.

You can tell how well a team's doing by the state of the wives. Second Division wives always need roots touching up.

MRS MERTON, played by Caroline Hook, on *The Mrs Merton Show*, BBC2, 1995.

John Hollins was a mistake. He has a very strong wife. It might have been better if I'd made her manager.

KEN BATES, Chelsea chairman, 1995.

I know he's got a domestic problem in that his girlfriend doesn't want to live in Birmingham. I've told him to change his girlfriend and not his club.

BARRY FRY, Birmingham manager, on his Portuguese winger Jose Dominguez,
who eventually joined Sporting Lisbon, 1993.

I can't play well knowing that she is upset. It's not as if she's a yokel.

STEVE YATES, QPR defender, on seeking a transfer because his wife
was taunted about her West Country accent, 1995.

Q: What has been your biggest thrill in life?
A: When my wife Norma told me she was pregnant and signing for Newcastle.

> ALBERT CRAIG, Partick Thistle midfielder, in *Sun* questionnaire, 1994.

Into him lads! He's vulnerable – his wife's leaving him!

> CHARACTER in *Atletico Partick AFC*, BBC-TV sitcom, 1995. The speaker
> was a footballing social worker who was discussing divorce with the
> main character, Jack Roan, when the ball came their way.

I just want to thank him. Our two boys are over the moon that United have won.

> SANDRA SEAMAN, ex-wife of Arsenal goalkeeper David Seaman,
> ringing Radio Hallam's phone-in after Sheffield United
> knocked the Gunners out of the FA Cup, 1996.

I loved football. I played in the morning and in the afternoon. Even when I went to bed with my wife I was training.

> DIEGO MARADONA, 1994.

No wonder that girl was licking his toes. She was probably trying to get as far away from his face as she possibly could.

> TOMMY DOCHERTY, broadcaster and former manager, on David Mellor MP,
> host of BBC Radio 5 Live's *Six-O-Six* phone-in, 1996.

Could you take Eric's sliding tackle from behind? Football. It's a girl's game.

> *DAILY STAR* advertisement, 1995. Other slogans for the same ad
> included 'Imagine Ruud pumping his balls into your box' and
> 'Ryan offers great penetration'.

I didn't get too many women running after me. It was their f****** husbands who'd be after me.

> CHARLIE GEORGE, former Arsenal and England player,
> recalling life at the top in the Seventies, 1995.

Every girlfriend I ever went out with I took (on the North Bank terracing) at least once. They never wanted to go twice.

> LAURENCE MARKS, comedy writer, in Tom Watt,
> *The End: 80 Years of Life on Arsenal's North Bank*, 1993.

The best-looking girl I know is my wife and that's the honest truth. But I can't say I think about that sort of thing very often.

RON ATKINSON, Coventry manager, asked by Loaded magazine
'what sort of women' he fancied, 1995.

Q: If you could date any woman who would it be?
A: My missus as I never see her now!

BARRY FRY, Birmingham manager, in programme questionnaire, 1996.

Give her the most romantic night ever...make her feel as though she's the most special person in your life...better than a dozen red roses...She couldn't ask for more. Take her to see Paris Saint-Germain versus Glasgow Celtic tonight!

ADVERTISEMENT in L'Equipe, 1995.

Q: What is the craziest request you've had from a fan?
A: A male fan once asked me for my wife's phone number and when my next away match was.

FRANCIS BENALI, Southampton defender, in response to Sun questionnaire, 1995.

Our husbands think we're shopping in Dublin.

BANNER held by Republic of Ireland fans in Portugal, 1995.

I'd stop working tomorrow if I became Paul (Peschisolido's) wife. I love what I do, but my place would be at home for him. I know that will come as a shock to people who assume I'm a feminist, but I'm an old-fashioned girl and I truly believe a wife should cook, clean and stay at home to look after the kids.

KARREN BRADY, Birmingham City managing director,
before her marriage to the Stoke striker, 1994.

Q: At home, when was the last time you ironed a shirt?
A: I pay my wife to do that.

MARK ROBINS, Leicester striker, in programme questionnaire, 1995.

I'll tell you straight away, before you ask me: I've never slept with a footballer, I've never gone to dinner with one, and I've never seen one naked in the dressing-room. Ok, we can start.

PAOLA FERRARI, Italian TV football presenter, at the start of an interview, 1994.

I KNOW I LOOK DIFFERENT ON THE OUTSIDE, BUT
INSIDE I'M TOUGH AND STREETWISE. I BELIEVE IN
FRONTING EVERYTHING OUT.

KARREN BRADY, Birmingham City managing director, 1995.

I met much more chauvinism when I was working for *The Sport*. I've always had the 'I bet she's shagging the boss' remarks.

KARREN BRADY, managing director of Birmingham City, 1995.

I know everybody thinks I earned this job between the sheets, but I'm not bonking him.

BRADY on her relationship with Birmingham's owner, David Sullivan, 1994.

I know people in the game prefer not to deal with me, because I am tough and uncompromising. Barry Fry can be like Father Christmas. I am the wicked stepmother.

BRADY, 1995.

CHAPTER 9

The Blazer Brigade

Industries go to the wall every day, look at Swan Hunter here in the North-east. I didn't hear too many cry for them, it was recognised they had to go. Football's a business, it's no different, and it's not going to be run by the blazer brigade any more. It needs to be run as a business by businessmen.

SIR JOHN HALL, Newcastle chairman, and advocate of a closed shop,
two-division Premier League, 1995.

Wolves, Derby, Blackburn: these fans with money pour it in, the club lights up, then it fizzles away. Doesn't work. End of story.

KEN BATES, Chelsea chairman, 1995.

For years I've been saying football should be run by football people, then along came Franny Lee at Manchester City. Oh well, back to the drawing board.

JIMMY GREAVES, in his *Sun* column, 1995.

If anyone asks, you have total control of team selection. You don't, of course. It's just that I'm fed up with being portrayed as a megalo-maniac.

CHAIRMAN, played by Timothy West, to caretaker manager
(James Bolam), in Channel 4 comedy drama
Eleven Men Against Eleven, 1995.

We could do without comments like that, especially from someone who doesn't know a goal-line from a clothes line.

> BARRY FRY, Birmingham manager, on criticism of his team
> by club owner David Sullivan, 1994.

Dreams are the thread that draw this whole industry together, from parks football to Carlisle to AC Milan. We all aspire to The Dream. Robert Maxwell dubbed me a Walter Mitty figure, but that's fine because this is the industry of dreams and I'm the greatest dreamer alive.

> MICHAEL KNIGHTON, Carlisle chairman and
> former Manchester United director, 1995.

I was stood on my seat in the directors' box. I was gone! When the final whistle went, they thrust me down the front. Eighteen thousand people were singing 'There's only one Bill Kenwright!' the next day I went out to Hampstead Heath and cried for three hours. I said: 'Never again.' My business went to pieces for those five months. My life went to pieces. That's the other side of being a director.

> BILL KENWRIGHT, Everton director and theatre impressario,
> on the club's last-gasp escape from relegation, 1994.

I don't agree with all these multi-millionaires coming into football. I still get the collywobbles every time I look up and see a helicopter.

> ALAN BUCKLEY, West Brom manager, looking back at the arrival from the skies
> of the man who eventually sacked him at Walsall, Terry Ramsden, 1995.

When my son (Jonathan, Wolves chairman) comes to me and asks for more money to buy another player, I tell him: 'This is blackmail'. Then he says: 'Do you want to get into the Premiership?' and I say: 'Yes'. Then he says: 'Do you want to win the FA Cup?' and I say: 'Yes'. And then I say: 'Oh, go and buy him then.'

> SIR JACK HAYWARD, Wolves' owner and president, 1995.

I'll keep throwing money at it until we get it right, or until the men in white coats wheel me away.

> SIR JACK HAYWARD, on his investment in the club,
> which then stood at £20m, 1993.

A friend has described me as the village vicar of football chairmen, which I rather like, but I have discovered there are people in the game who would slit your throat for tuppence. People with more experience than us tried to take advantage of our naivety.

> JONATHAN HAYWARD, Wolves chairman, son of Sir Jack,
> and Northumberland farmer, 1995.

I have a sister and a brother who must be thinking: 'What is happening to our money?' They're seeing their inheritance slipping away before their eyes. They wonder when it is all going to end.

> JONATHAN HAYWARD on Sir Jack's £35m outlay on stadium
> redevelopment and players, 1995.

People say: 'You must have better things to spend your money on'. But I've no desire for huge yachts in Monte Carlo. I'm just a homely boy from East Northants who enjoys doing what I do.

> MAX GRIGGS, chairman of Rushden & Diamonds and of the Doc Martens footwear empire,
> on ploughing £10m-plus into the non-league club, 1995.

I put a few hundred thousand in, not a lot. And that's it – there's no more where that came from. I've told everyone I ain't Jack Walker. It's a relatively straightforward thing to go out, spend £50m and buy a good team. You could put your house on it, if we did, that we'd be promoted from the Third Division this season. But I ain't going to. I'm a chartered accountant. On the opposite side of my heart is my wallet. This is a business for me. I can't score the goals, but I can look after the accounts. That's how I get my buzz.

> BARRY HEARN, boxing and snooker promoter,
> on taking over Third Division Leyton Orient, 1995.

People say you can't do this, you can't do that. I say: 'Just watch me. I'm a genius'. There's no way I won't make money.

> BARRY HEARN, 1995.

I don't think the late Sir John Moores would have liked to have seen the Everton team becoming an outpost of Manchester. I think it is important that our Merseyside clubs are controlled from within Merseyside and run by Merseysiders.

> PETER JOHNSON, Tranmere chairman, claiming that the rival consortium
> bidding to take over Everton were Manchester-based, 1994.

The cynics on Merseyside will say: 'How can he have any sentiment when he has supported Tranmere, Everton and Liverpool?' But I'm as committed to Everton now as I ever was to the other two. I didn't put £10m into the club not to be committed.

JOHNSON, by now Everton chairman, 1994.

I wonder if Johnson has mentioned he is a Liverpool supporter who has been a season ticket holder at Anfield. The Moores children were charged by their father with the task of making sure the club went into good hands, and by that he didn't mean he wanted it to go to a Liverpudlian.

PROFESSOR TOM CANNON, spokesman for the rival Bill Kenwright group, 1994.

You saved the club. Now you must get control, and make sure everybody who wants a piece of the action, whoever they are, pays for everything.

SIR JOHN HALL, Newcastle chairman giving advice to Celtic owner Fergus McCann, 1995.

The director's role of Ron Noades at Crystal Palace increasingly defines all that is wrong with the way certain English football clubs are run.

JOHN GILES, former Leeds captain and ex-manager, 1995.

Peter Swales wore a wig, a blazer with an England badge on it, and high-heeled shoes. As a man he really impressed me.

MALCOLM ALLISON, ex-Manchester City manager, on the club's former chairman
in Jeremy Novick, In A League of Their Own: Football's Maverick Managers, 1995.

I have been praying all week and will keep praying that Mr Swales will leave.

REVEREND JIM BURNS, Vicar of St Peter's, Manchester, on his part in the
'Forward With Franny Lee' campaign, 1995.

Death threats against me are one thing, but when supporters will sink to the depths of involving an 87-year-old woman I think the time has come to take action.

PETER SWALES, resigning as City chairman following an alleged incident
in his mother's retirement home, 1994.

I'm very fortunate that the pressure doesn't have the same effect on me as it has on other people. I've been in local government and politics for 30 years and involved in much more heated scenes in debates on closing village schools or hospital wards.

> ROBERT CHASE, Norwich chairman, on demonstrations
> against him by supporters, 1995.

At home we talk about Christmas presents and next year's summer holiday. What we don't talk about is what's happening at Carrow Road.

> CHASE, 1995.

If (the protests) bothered me, would I not be hiding in a bunker? When I went to sleep afterwards my head hit the pillow and I knew nothing more until someone brought me a cup of tea at 7.30am.

> CHASE, 1995.

Death To The Fat Controller

> NORWICH fanzine title, 1995.

Robert Chases's Ambitions – R.I.P.

> SIGN on coffin carried by Norwich fans, 1995.

Amstrad's got £150m sitting in the bank that we don't know what to do with. That doesn't mean I can get a cheque book out and start spending money like a hooligan.

> ALAN SUGAR, Tottenham chairman, 1994.

He (Sugar) is behaving disgracefully and without honour. It is clear he does not remember the contracts he signs. I don't understand what there is to discuss here. Everything is laid down in black and white. The English fans showed me the meaning of fair play in their country, but the man who signed the contract is leading me away from that opinion.

> JURGEN KLINSMANN after returning to Bayern Munich, 1995.

I make this promise. If there's any more abuse to either myself or my family, that will be it.

> SUGAR, 1995.

I can't believe the way Sugar has got upset with the fans. It's hilarious. He wants to be loved. It's pure ego. But fans get agitated if things go wrong. I've had aggro in a different league to the ones moaning about Sugar. What you don't do is descend to their level. You give them a smile and blow 'em a kiss. That kills them.

> BARRY HEARN, Leyton Orient owner, on his neighbour's
> travails at Tottenham, 1995.

Ken Bates here. I understand you're richer than I am, so we'd better get together.

> KEN BATES, Chelsea chairman, in phone call to wealthy supporter Matthew Harding, 1994.
> Harding was to put in £24m over the next two years.

I wouldn't say I was interested in football generally. It's all Chelsea as far as I'm concerned.

> MATTHEW HARDING, Chelsea director and multi-millionaire, 1995.

It will at least stop the embarrassment in the boardroom of the behaviour related to your heavy drinking both home and away.

> BATES' letter banning Harding, 1995.

Please ensure that your 'Bates Out' banner in the North Stand does not obscure the valuable advertisement panels in the upper tier.

> P.S. TO BATES' letter. The ban was subsequently rescinded.

I've been watching Chelsea from outside the directors' box for 31 of the past 33 years, so this ban is hardly going to kill me.

> MATTHEW HARDING, 1995.

He's been very nice to my face while at the same time courting young journalists, the ones who are impressed with being courted by a rich young man. What he hasn't realised is that almost step by step everything he's been doing has been reported back to me.

> BATES on Harding, 1995.

It has taken us a year not to get a reply. All we have is fluff on the capuccino.

> BATES on a breakdown of communication with Harding, 1995.

So what? Ninety-nine per cent of all Iraqis voted for Saddam Hussein.

BATES on being informed that a poll showed Chelsea fans
wanted Harding to replace him, 1995.

I don't give a damn about being chairman. All I know is that at the moment we have the wrong chairman.

HARDING, 1995.

The difference is that Bates appears to think it is his club, while Harding's attitude is that it is our club.

ROSS FRASER, chairman of Chelsea Independent Supporters' Association, 1995.

When David Mellor is prepared to put money into the club – or even pay for his own tickets – he will be entitled to his opinion.

HARDING answering criticism by the Conservative MP and football phone-in host, 1995.

It was nice to see them sitting together. I don't know whether they were holding hands or not.

GLENN HODDLE, Chelsea manager, on a thaw in relations between Bates and Harding, 1995.

The board at Southampton are excellent. They sacked me and, yes, I'd like to prove them wrong, but they put up with me for six years. That was long enough for anybody. They wanted a change and they were right to do it.

CHRIS NICHOLL, Walsall manager, recalling his sacking by Southampton, 1996.

If anyone thinks we're going to give away a company which we've built up over six years at a personal loss to satisfy the wishes of some Indian with a curry shop, they'd better get real.

JIM OLIVER, chairman, Partick Thistle, on spurning a takeover bid
by a consortium of Asian businessmen, 1995.

We'd deal with anyone, whether they were Asian, Eskimo, one-eyed black lesbian saxophone player.

OLIVER, denying allegations of racism, 1995.

I won't have a trades union man telling me who I can or cannot employ in my own country.

SIR JOHN HALL, Newcastle chairman, on Gordon Taylor's (players' union chief)
fears about foreign players in English football, 1995.

I take £120,000 a year, plus expenses. You can't get a good player for that, let alone a financial genius.

KEN BATES, Chelsea chairman, 1995.

If you had taken £150,000 out of the club in consultancy fees and a further £100,000 in expenses over a 12-month period, you would want back into the game, wouldn't you?

CHRIS ROBINSON, Heart of Midlothian chairman, on suggestions that his predecessor, Wallace Mercer, planned to return to the game, 1995.

I used to think the construction industry was bent but I was shocked by what I saw in other football clubs. Football seems to be bent from top to bottom.

DAVID KOHLER, Luton chairman, 1993.

I've survived two heart-attacks and Stan Flashman. And Stan was the worst of the three.

BARRY FRY, Birmingham manager, on his turbulent relationship with the Barnet chairman, 1995.

Mr Whelan is a god and our father in England. He is a very good person and, with him, Wigan will be in the First Division in two years.

ROBERTO MARTINEZ, one of three Spanish players recruited by Wigan owner and ex-Blackburn defender Dave Whelan, 1995.

I used to have to tour when I didn't really want to, to be able to afford to buy a centre-forward.

ELTON JOHN, pop artist and former Watford chairman, 1995.

The board here have been loyal to me. When I arrived they said there'd be no money and they've kept their promise.

DAVE BASSETT, Sheffield United manager, 1994.

The biggest disaster today is that they've lost the corkscrew for my red wine.

LIONEL BALL, chairman, Gravesend & Northfleet, after FA Cup victory over Colchester, 1995.

I don't want Wolves fans to think I'm off my trolley, but Dermot Reeve (Warwickshire cricket captain) is the kind of character I'm looking for as manager.

JONATHAN HAYWARD, chairman, Wolverhampton Wanderers, 1995.

Martin Edwards (the Manchester United chairman) told me they would be sending their first team out at York. I told him 'so will we'.

DOUGLAS CRAIG, York City chairman, after his team's 3-0 victory at Old Trafford
in the Coca-Cola Cup second round, first leg, 1995.
United won the return 3-1 but lost on aggregate.

If I'd known that the chairman (Doug Ellis) wasn't coming, we'd have come out on Saturday night.

RON ATKINSON, Aston Villa manager, arriving in Slovakia
on a Tuesday for a Uefa Cup tie, 1993.

We now live in the age of the high-profile chairman. He wants power, glory, prestige. He even wants to run the game. Yet these are the people who took us into the InterTwoBob Cup.

JIMMY GREAVES, 1995.

Many of these people have ruled over the decline of the game. We are now 23rd in the world rankings. If soccer had been like a business, they would have been out of their jobs a long time ago.

SIR JOHN HALL, Newcastle chairman on the FA Councillors, 1995.

I firmly believed that at the time, but now we live in a commercial world.

SIR BERT MILLICHIP, FA chairman, explaining why the FA had sold the FA Cup to sponsors
when he had previously described it as 'sacrosanct', 1994.

I'm shocked and disgusted. It's typical of the FA. They're worse than the Masons, and I don't think much of Masons.

ALAN THORNE, former Millwall chairman, on the FA's decision to suspend George Graham for a
year over the 'bung' allegations, 1995.

We've got grounds which are State of the Art and administration which is State of the Arc.

GORDON TAYLOR, PFA chief executive, on the 'bumbling'
investigation into the 'bung' scandal, 1995.

Go back to the golf course, breed horses, sail round the world, book a trip to the moon, but leave the rule book of our sport to us.

GUIDO TOGNONI, FIFA press officer, open letter to Franz Beckenbauer, 1994.

CHAPTER 10

Famous Last Words

I don't mind if we pick up a few yellow cards. I'm looking for a team which fights. No more nicey-nicey football.

> STEVEN McMAHON, Swindon player-manager, before being sent off
> on his debut for elbowing a Southend player, 1994.

I'm waiting for Desailly – I excel myself against blacks.

> HRISTO STOICHKOV, Barcelona's Bulgarian striker, before European Cup final, 1994.
> Milan won 4-0 and Marcel Desailly scored.

There are no easy games in the Premiership...apart from Ipswich at home.

> ALAN SHEARER, Blackburn striker, on learning that Manchester United
> had beaten Ipswich 9-0, 1995. Within a year, Ipswich beat
> Blackburn away in the FA Cup.

That's a home win and an away draw inside four days. We've only got one more game in November, and if we win that I'm in grave danger of ending up as manager of the month.

> MIKE WALKER, Everton manager, after draw at Norwich, 1994.
> He was sacked four days later.

We're becoming very difficult to beat.

> FRANK CLARK, Nottingham Forest manager, on his team's long unbeaten
> Premiership run, 1995. The day the interview was published,
> Forest lost 7-0 at Blackburn.

Rumours of my impending resignation have proved somewhat premature. After the Leicester game I was amazed to be asked whether I was going to resign on Monday. I was more interested in discussing the game. Anyway, that's another rumour squashed. I haven't finished spending and I have cash available for signings.

GEORGE GRAHAM programme column on the day of his dismissal
as Arsenal manager, 1995.

I believe Ron to be one of the top three managers in the country.

DOUG ELLIS, Aston Villa chairman, giving Ron Atkinson
a vote of confidence – three weeks before sacking him, 1994.

Regarding the recent speculation concerning myself and Aston Villa F.C. I wish to make it clear that I will not be the next manager of Aston Villa...I've had no approach from them and I've no idea what my plans are. It's time to do something different with my life, though I intend to stay in football.

BRIAN LITTLE, resigning as Leicester manager but denying an imminent move to
Villa Park, 1994. Four days later he took over as Villa manager.

So 12 months on I have no regrets at all about leaving Reading to become Leicester City manager. I knew I wouldn't. Here's to the next 12 months – and a return to the Premiership.

MARK McGHEE, Leicester manager, in December issue of club's *Blue Army News*, 1995.
Within days of its publication he had defected to Wolves.

I have always been happy here and ultimately I just couldn't give that up.

JIM JEFFRIES, Falkirk manager, on turning down the Hearts job, 1995.
Two days later he was confirmed as Hearts manager.

At least I'll be able to sleep tonight.

HOWARD KENDALL, Everton manager, after victory over Southampton, 1993.
An hour later, Kendall resigned.

We hope he will see this club through to the next century.

PETER SWALES, Manchester City chairman, when Peter Reid
signed three-year contract in February, 1993.
By September, Reid was sacked.

I would like to take this opportunity to speak directly to you, the supporters, about my relationship with the chairman, Peter Swales. Our relationship has always been healthy. We have had healthy discussions about the purchase of players...I have no problems.

REID in programme column the day before Swales ousted him.

We are not doing well. And that is down to me. The buck stops here.

REID in his programme column – written for a game played the day after his dismissal.

Birmingham haven't spoken to me or my chairman. If they do, yeah, I'll talk to them to see what it's all about. But I'm as happy as a sandboy here. At last I'm at what I call a proper football club. I've got reserves, a youth team – everything I ever wanted.

BARRY FRY, Southend manager, 1993. A week later he had joined Birmingham amid bitterness and legal wrangling.

If (Alan) Sugar thinks he can just walk in and take West Brom's manager, I'll be down the motorway in my car like an Exocet and blow up his bloody computers.

TREVOR SUMMERS, West Bromwich Albion chairman, on Spurs' interest in Ossie Ardiles, 1993. Ardiles duly joined Spurs.

Ardiles had a four-year contract when he signed with Spurs and that contract will be observed. He has the backing of the board and if we're in the First Division next season he will be our manager to start the season off.

ALAN SUGAR, Tottenham chairman, during bad start to 1994-95. Ardiles was sacked in October.

I like Nottingham. It's a bit like Ireland. My heart is with this club. My present contract has another year to go, and I did have another one of three years in mind, but now I fancy something a bit longer.

ROY KEANE denying he would leave Nottingham Forest if they were relegated January, 1993. He left in July.

I'm from the North and you do miss it. But that was blown out of all proportion really. I'm delighted to be staying for another four years.

NICK BARMBY, England striker, on signing a new contract with Tottenham – five months before joining Middlebrough, 1995.

Moving back to the Bundesliga would be boring.

> JURGEN KLINSMANN, Tottenham striker, four months before returning
> to Germany with Bayern Munich, 1995.

I'd walk across broken glass to join the club.

> GEOFF THOMAS, Crystal Palace midfielder, on the interest of his boyhood heroes,
> Manchester City, 1993. He promptly signed for Wolves.

Ince is just not for sale. I'm absolutely adamant about that.

> ALEX FERGUSON, Manchester United manager, denying his midfielder's imminent move
> to Inter Milan, 1995. Within two weeks the deal had gone through.

Oh, you're certain to win the league now.

> LES KERSHAW, Manchester United chief scout, to manager Alex Ferguson
> on hearing that United were signing Andy Cole, 1995.

I don't believe Romario will cause any more problems than somebody like Alan Shearer, or Ian Rush.

> STEVE BRUCE, Manchester United captain, returning to the side for United's
> second match with Barcelona, 1994. Barcelona won 4-0.

Playing in 130 degrees is exhausting – even for a keeper. People tell me I should be OK since I can keep a carton of water in the net. But I have this nightmare vision of me standing on the line, downing a pint of water as a 60-yard shot sails past me.

> PACKIE BONNER, Republic of Ireland goalkeeper, writing in a Scottish newspaper 24 hours
> before his costly error v The Netherlands, World Cup finals, 1994.

The players are under no pressure to get a result, so you never know what might happen.

> TOMMY GEMMELL, Albion Rovers manager, before 11-0 defeat
> by Partick Thistle, Scottish Cup, 1994.

A referee who has to use a red card to control a match is a weak referee.

> GUNTER WIESEL, German referee, three days before sending off five players in a Borussia
> Dortmund v Dynamo Dresden match, 1994.

Current form counts for nothing when United play City.

> GARRY FLITCROFT, Manchester City captain, 1995. City had not beaten United
> for seven years, and duly lost again.

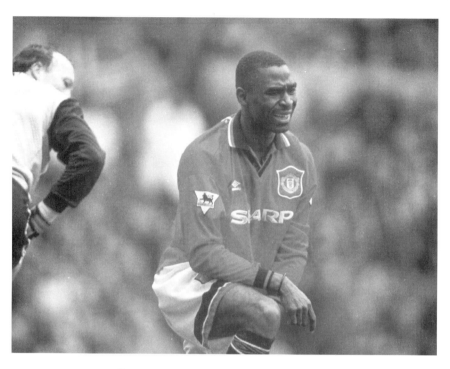

I WILL SCORE LOADS OF GOALS HERE.

ANDY COLE signing for Manchester United, 1995.

CARPENTER'S SON ZELJKO CAN BE NEW CITY MESSIAH!

BLUE ARMY NEWS, Leicester City newspaper headline, 1995. Zeljko Kalac,
a 6ft 7in Australian goalkeeper, was dropped and offered to Wolves
after two first-team appearances.

Whatever the scoreline after 90 minutes' play, the players, directors, staff and of course supporters of Kidderminster will have had a terrific day out.

BIRMINGHAM programme's welcome to Kidderminster Harriers
before FA Cup tie, 1994. The non-Leaguers won 2-1.

I think I've only had a couple of bookings in the last dozen games, which is good for me. I better not say any more about that or I'll probably be sent off tonight.

ROY KEANE, Republic of Ireland midfielder, in Dublin's *Evening Herald*
before he was dismissed v Russia, 1996.

Ideally, I'd like to pop my clogs puching the air celebrvj^r g Blues' winning goal at Wembley in the year 2130.

BARRY FRY envisaging the length of his stay as Birmingham manager
shortly before dismissal, 1996.

If we don't get voted in, I'll go bungee jumping without the rope.

MATT HALL, Gala Fairydean chairman, on how he would react if his club
were not elected to the Scottish League, 1994. They failed.

If Shearer plays for England, so can I.

SPURS FANS' SONG at Blackburn during Shearer's long barren run
at international level, 1995. Within minutes, Shearer struck his
100th Premiership goal from 25 yards.

My watch is tops! With its classy design and easy-to-read watch face, I am never late for training or Blues games!

STEVE CLARIDGE, Birmingham striker, on the virtues of the club wrist-watch, 1996.
His endorsement appeared in the programme after he was fined for arriving late
at Crystal Palace and his subsequent transfer to Leicester.

This is where Kenny will come into his own. He will fulfil his role as Director of Football and be our European envoy. No one knows the Continental scene better.

RAY HARFORD, Blackburn manager, after draw for European Cup Champions' League, 1995. Blackburn finished bottom of their group, with Dalglish conspicuously uninvolved.

Through football we're trying to show that Colombia is about more than cocaine, violence, terrorism and death.

FRANCISCO MATURANA, Colombia coach, on eve of World Cup finals, during which his centre-back Andres Escobar was shot dead, 1994.

CHAPTER 11

Euro '96
And All That

It's coming home, it's coming home
It's coming, football's coming home

ENGLAND SQUAD pop song featuring David Baddiel, Frank Skinner
and the Lightning Seeds – and the Wembley 75,000.

You've got to have a happy squad. While preparations have got to be right it's not compulsory to be bored out of your head.

TERRY VENABLES defending England's pre-tournament trip to the Far East.

ENGLAND ACES BACK ON THE BOOZE

SUN headline alleging players drank in a nightclub
until 2.20am after opening draw v Switzerland.

If you drink heavily it can be very difficult to rehydrate properly, and the recent hot weather will not have helped. Even two or three pints of beer in an evening is enough to cause problems.

Dr RICHARD BUDGETT, director of medical services,
British Olympic Association, on England's apparent lack of fitness.

Beer is not a diuretic and can help the rehydration process. I would not be unhappy with the players having a couple of beers.

RON MAUGHAM, Professor of Human Physiology at Aberdeen University
and adviser to the British Olympic team.

It's Bavarian state law that beer isn't alcohol. It's a means of nutrition.

JURGEN KLINSMANN on the 'boozy England' furore.

The players feel there are people who are being traitors to us. These people are turning the public against the players, which can then turn the fans against the players inside the stadium. It seems everything is very negative against the players, who have only got themselves.

TERRY VENABLES on the complaints about his players' drinking.

The Guvnor, as Paul Ince likes to call himself, couldn't order a meal on last week's evidence.

ALAN HUDSON, former England midfielder,
on England's faltering start.

Stoichkov does not know how to play fair. He plays for fouls by putting his shoulder in and then falling down. He uses the elbow too. We do not like him.

JAVIER CLEMENTE, Spain coach, after Spain 1 Bulgaria 1.

Dennis (Bergkamp) is such a nice man, such a tremendous gentleman, with such a lovely family - it's going to be very hard for me to kick him.

TONY ADAMS, England captain, on his Arsenal colleague
and Dutch opponent.

Players should not content themselves with wearing fair play logos, but are also expected to display fair play in their conduct.

LENNART JOHANSSON, UEFA President.

There are two possibilities from this tournament. Either I shall be kissed all over my bald head or I will have tomatoes thrown at it.

ARRIGO SACCHI, Italy coach.

The trouble with Sacchi is he thinks he's God.

ITALIAN JOURNALIST after Italy 2 Russia 1.

You simply don't change a winning side, do you? And given that the players seemed to me in generally good shape, there remains only one explanation: Sacchi overrated himself. I get the impression that he wanted to prove he is more important than the players.

GIANNI RIVERA on Sacchi's five changes v Czech Republic.
The Czechs won 2–1.

If I had been on the bench after scoring two goals, I would have found it hard to accept.

> JURGEN KLINSMANN on Sacchi dropping Casiraghi against the Czechs.

I have all the best players here tactically and technically, but I made the mistake of not considering their morale, spirit and mental preparedness. This is something that gives me a headache.

> OLEG ROMANTSEV, Russia coach, before game against Czech Republic.

A goalkeeper is a goalkeeper because he can't play football.

> RUUD GULLIT, BBC-TV pundit, after Russia's Stanislav Cherchesov gifted Italy a goal.

He doesn't know whether it's New Year or New York.

> MARK LAWRENSON, Radio Five Live, on Apolloni, Italian defender,
> as Nedved scored for Czech Republic.

Everything's through the middle - they've less width than Bernard Manning.

> LAWRENSON on the Portuguese.

Three days before this match, on the strength of Holland's victory over Ireland, they were supposed to be the best team in the world. The press in England were saying this was the way the English game should go, that it's the game of the future. Well, we've got a draw and they can moan all night if they like.

> JOHN SPENCER, Scotland forward, on Dutch complaints
> after Scotland 0 Holland 0.

The English are so arrogant, they still think they are the best in the world.

> SPENCER before England v Scotland four days later.

Gary McAllister is the metronome - he makes them play quicker or slower, and also scores many free-kicks.

> DENNIS BERGKAMP, Holland striker, on Scotland.

I hope Saturday's display has enhanced my claim to be regarded as the World's No 1.

> DAVID SEAMAN after saving Gary McAllister's penalty, England 2 Scotland 0.

Hitting it straight is not something I usually do, but given the stage of the game I felt I had to score.

> GARY McALLISTER explaining his change of style for that penalty.

(Gazza) is no longer a fat, drunken imbecile...he is in fact a football genius.

> DAILY MIRROR editorial headed 'Mr Paul Gascoigne:
> An Apology', after his goal v Scotland.

Gazza went berserk. He was shouting 'Yes!' at the top of his voice plus some things that were unprintable.

> DAVID SEAMAN, England goalkeeper, after win v Scotland.

I think Gascoigne might have a problem with extra time.

> FRANZ BECKENBAUER on the England player's fitness.

What am I to think when the coach (Guus Hiddink) has his hands and head up the backside of certain players?

> EDGAR DAVIDS, Dutch midfielder. Hiddink sent him home after one game.

It wouldn't be a major tournament if there wasn't talk of rows and disagreements in the Dutch camp.

> RUUD GULLIT, former Dutch captain, on Davids' exit.

Apparently, the future is not orange.

> D, singer with pop group Massive Attack,
> after England's rout of the Dutch.

Forty thousand Englishmen can't be wrong.

> BRIAN MOORE, ITV commentator, complaining
> about England v Holland referee.

England's victory over Holland has sparked a nationwide 'feelgood factor' that may make us all better lovers, experts said yesterday.

> SUN news story.

I've always believed we could be as good as Brazil.

> TEDDY SHERINGHAM, England striker, after 4-1 win over Holland.

I KNOW THERE ARE FAR MORE IMPORTANT THINGS IN LIFE THAN FOOT-
BALL, BUT IF YOU CUT ME OPEN AND HAD A LOOK INSIDE RIGHT NOW IT
WOULDN'T BE A PRETTY SIGHT. I DON'T KNOW IF I CAN SINK ANY LOWER.

GARY McALLISTER, Scotland captain, after Seaman had saved his penalty.

When Patrick Kluivert scored it was the same feeling as when Mel Gibson got hung, drawn and quartered at the end of *Braveheart*.

DOMINIK DIAMOND, broadcaster and Scotland fan,
after late Dutch goal v England eliminated the Scots.

12-page Scotland Agony Special – in colour!

DAILY RECORD billboards after Scots' exit.

We seem to be stuck on the 'Inger-lund, Inger-lund, Inger-lund' chant. That may be a bit boring but at least everybody knows the words.

HELEN JOSLIN, Football Supporters' Association official.

I've been to four World Cups and four European Championships, and this is the first time any one has tried to keep me out.

MANOLO, the Spanish fan with the big bass drum, after being refused entry to Spain v Bulgaria.

Let's face it, Manolo's drum is bigger than the average drum. To an English fan, if a bloody great drum got stuck in front of you, you'd be upset. But the continentals are used to that, so it's not a problem.

JOHN PENTITH, Leeds Police, after the authorites allowed Manolo in.

Both sets of fans find the coffee and soup undrinkable in Leeds, so they have no choice but to drink beer.

24 CHASA caption to picture of Spanish and Bulgarian fans drinking together.

Leeds United's idea of welcoming Spanish fans has been to play endless Julio Iglesias records over the PA.

SPOKESMAN at FSA 'embassy' in Leeds.

Where's the beach?

PORTUGAL FANS at FSA 'embassy'...in Sheffield.

English grass simply invites you to walk on it, to run on it or even throw yourself on it. I've decided to grow it in front of my house at home.

MARIJAN MRMIC, Croatia goalkeeper.

Training has been cancelled. They have the day off and are planning a shopping spree in Wigan.

LEV ZARAKHOVICH, Russian press officer.

They are both world class, but you cannot compare the two. You could say Davor is a romantic footballer, but Jurgen is a modern footballer.

MIROSLAV BLAZEVIC, Croatia coach, on Klinsmann and Suker.

Jurgen is a goalscoring machine. He used to get so frustrated if he wasn't scoring he would bang his head on the door. Davor doesn't do that!

OTTO BARIC, Croatia assistant coach, comparing Klinsmann, whom he coached at Stuttgart as a teenager, and Suker.

We're eating British beef and it's perfectly all right. It can't be doing us too much harm because we've won twice already.

WOLFGANG NIERSBACH, German Press Officer, as 'mad cow' debate raged.

Not only the cows are mad in England. The English press is also infected.

EL MUNDO DEPORTIVO newspaper, after 'Spain-bashing' stories before quarter-final.

There will be 2,000 of our fans against 70,000 drunkards.

JAVIER CLEMENTE, Spain coach, before facing England.

The Germans are very well behaved, more like a lawyers' convention than a squad of footballers.

JEFF BURNIGE, German team liaison officer and Millwall director.

I was very disappointed with the Germans physically. Everyone thinks they are big and strong and have superior physiques, but they were so weak.

SLAVEN BILIC, Croatia defender, after the sour quarter-final.

I couldn't say it was the most physical game of the tournament - but it was certainly above average.

MATTHIAS SAMMER, German sweeper, after the Croatia game.

Half the team are foreigners who don't even know the words to the Marseillaise.

JEAN-MARIE LE PEN, French fascist leader, criticising France's team.

Me sing to satisfy Le Pen? I don't think so.

MARCEL DESAILLY, black French defender.

Could you ask Gascoigne to show a bit of respect and stand up when the other team's national anthem is being played. There are other times when he can bend down and do his socks, jump around and stretch. It is disrespectful.

JAVIER CLEMENTE, Spain coach.

I recognised Gascoigne's medieval hair and portly stomach, and Tony Adams' long, strong legs.

A.S.BYATT, author, on her first football match.

Radek Bejbl is like Carlton Palmer without the skill.

RACING POST before the Czech player's winner and Man of the Match award v Italy.

The organisers are not too happy with the fact that we have advanced. We are a negative attraction.

FRANTISEKH CHVALOVSKY, Czech FA president, before the semi-final.

We want patriotism, not hate. It's a football match, not a war.

VENABLES before England v Germany semi-final.

I've only taken one penalty before, for Crystal Palace at Ipswich. It was 2-2 in the 89th minute, I hit the post and we went down that year. But I think I'd be far more comfortable now than I was then.

GARETH SOUTHGATE, England defender, tempting fate before his decisive miss in semi-final shoot-out v Germany.

Don't worry, the next six years will fly by.

STUART PEARCE to Southgate.

Why didn't you just belt it?

BARBARA SOUTHGATE to her son.

It is loading a bullet into the chamber of a gun and asking everyone to pull the trigger. Someone will get the bullet, you know that. And it will reduce them to nothing. Fair? Fairness is not even an issue.

CHRISTIAN KAREMBEU, France midfielder, on the penalty shoot-out.

Q: What do you admire most about Germany?
A: Their results.

VENABLES at his last England press conference.

Overall the best tcam in the tournament has now been crowned as European champions.

BERTI VOGTS, Germany coach, after 2–1 win over Czech Republic in the final.

Index